LESBIAN MOTHERS

Dr. Alona Peleg

Production by eBookPro Publishing
www.ebook-pro.com

LESBIAN MOTHERS
Dr. Alona Peleg

Translation from Hebrew: Sarah Winkler
Editing: Dalia Talmon

Contact: peleg.alona@gmail.com

ISBN 9798336874853

LESBIAN MOTHERS

Overcoming the Challenges of Same-Sex Parenting

DR. ALONA PELEG

The book is dedicated with love and respect
to my mother, *Esther Colber Flink*,
her memory blessed, and to my father, *Shmuel Flink*,
will be distinguished for a long life.

Special thanks to *Ethi*, my beloved partner,
and *Yuval* and *Shira*, my precious children,
the gifts of my life.

Contents

A PERSONAL NOTE

This book has been building up inside me for many years. It was written with love and compassion for the girl I was at 14 who was astonished to discover that she had intimate feelings for one of her best girlfriends. With the love for that young, confused girl, whom no one had prepared for that moment and who was helpless, ashamed, fearful and dreading her future.

It had a name – she knew that – a name loaded with so many negative connotations that she didn't want to be identified with. That girl who in adulthood had wed and divorced a man, and summoned the courage to walk an unpaved, controversial, and fragile path, and start a family and raise two children with a woman.

This journey called for considerable effort and courage, investigation, skepticism, questioning, and abandoning of those common "truths" telling us "gays and lesbians are not normal, a family consists of a man and a woman," "children need a father," and so on. That journey called for 'unlearning' – forgetting, resisting, and questioning all that previous knowledge I've been taught, taking a deep breath, and saying, "That belief is wrong" and "That belief is oppressive."

It required looking into the eyes of my beloved parents and telling them things they didn't want to hear, which they found extremely difficult to understand and accept, risking losing what is the most precious to me of all, their love. In the end, they passed the toughest parenting test I ever put them through –

loving me unconditionally. And to this day, their love, their trust in me and their support is my source of strength and inspiration.

This book is an adaptation of my doctoral thesis. It offers a glimpse into the lives of the first generation in Israel of women in planned same-sex families. It was written with the utmost respect for these women, wishing to present and make heard the voices of those who are invisible or voiceless in the Israeli heterosexual society. Along with the extraordinary power of these trailblazing women and the strengths of same-sex parenting, it also outlines the suffering, difficulties, stressors and unique challenges faced by them and their children.

In writing and publishing this book, I am performing a double subversive act – first, in showcasing the way lesbian women are canceled, ignored and silenced by the general heterosexual society; and secondly, in shattering the silence and self-silencing that lesbian women in general, and lesbian mothers in particular, impose on themselves in order to be accepted, belong and desired.

In the current politics of neoliberal sexual rights (Duggan, 2003), the calculation of many parents in same-sex families is frigid and cruel. In order to gain equal rights, we have to be as akin, ordinary, and normative as possible. Any sign of difference or expression of hardship can be used as ammunition by those who believe we are undeserving of equal rights.

Yet, I believe that this strategy is a double-edged sword, dismantling us from within, suppressing any trace of uniqueness and creativity, and weakening us in the long run. It traps us in an endless discourse of defensiveness and self-justification, which offers renewed validity to accusations against us. It seems to me that the time is ripe to speak out about our difficulties and unique needs, and to demand recognition, legitimacy and an improved response, from all national systems- law, justice, health, education and welfare, for us and for our children.

Here is hoping that decision makers, policy makers, educators, and therapists all around the world, will use the information and recommendations detailed in this book, to learn about the experiences of parents and children of same-sex families, to initiate change in their social conditions so as to improve these families' quality of life and mental well-being. I have a dream that every teenage boy or girl, who are wondering about being lesbian or gay, asking themselves what future awaits them, will know that it is their right to be who they are, to love and choose their partner, and build a family, for a meaningful, satisfying and quality future which awaits them.

Acknowledgments

I would like to sincerely thank the people who made a significant contribution in bringing this book to the world:

Professor Tova Hartman from Ono Academic College and Professor Rachel Ben-Ari from Bar-Ilan University, for their guidance during the writing and processing of this doctoral thesis; to Professor Orly Benjamin of Bar-Ilan University for her inspiration and valuable advice; to the Levinsky-Wingate Academic College, my academic and professional home of inquiry, deepening and development; to Dr. Itzhak Benyamini and Idan Zivoni, editors of Resling Publishing, for their trust, guidance and support, and for providing me the means to realize my dream and publish the book; to Stavit Sinai for professional, sensitive and enlightening content editing, to Michal Pe'er, senior editor, for her vital recommendations, and to Kinneret Luria, for her linguistic editing. Warm thanks to the people of eBok Pro Publishing for their help in translating the book into English, editing and publishing the book

A special thanks to the dear and brave women who opened their doors and hearts, and shared their life stories with me.

INTRODUCTION

I, at age thirty-seven, and my partner at forty-four, had lived long adult lives marked by difference, marked by marginalization, which we both resisted and embraced. Becoming parents required something else of us; we were expected to put on a kind of normality that felt like someone else's skin [...] At first, I was delighted by this new sense of belonging, by how my life suddenly made sense to just about everyone. But as time went on, I felt less and less intelligible to myself. It was as if my life split and doubled. On the one hand, I became a symbol for normality and a vehicle through which liberal heterosexuals could reaffirm their own tolerance, their willingness to see me as the same. On the other hand, I recognized with excruciating clarity that real sameness requires no special celebration, does not evoke a special kind of attention (Mann, 2007: 152).

American researcher Bonnie Mann (2007) used these words to describe how she felt the moment she became a lesbian mother. She used the metaphor of splitting and the image of feeling in "someone else's skin" to describe her mixed emotions of pleasure, belonging and sameness on the one hand, and confusion, loss of way and alienation on the other, in relation to the normalization processes.

For three decades, lesbian women in Israel have been raising children in planned same-sex fatherless families. Planned same-sex families are families in which a same-sex childless couple make the transition to parenthood. Throughout human history, lesbian women have been "pre-blamed" with mental pathologies, moral inferiority and parental incompetence.[1] These transition to motherhood and family life encourages normalization processes and helps these women advance from the social margins toward the center.

This book attempts to examine the significance of the transition of Jewish lesbian women in Israel to motherhood and family life, from these women's perspective; how they interpret, translate and reformulate their identity and social standing. Moreover, the book addresses the difficulties, pressures and unique challenges they face, and their ways of coping and adapting.

This book is based on extensive research which I conducted between the years 2009–2016.[2] The term "minority stress" describes the experience of increased stress experienced by those with different sexual orientations as a consequence of belonging to a social group with a stigma (Meyer, 1995, 2003). As a woman raising her children with a partner in a planned same-sex fatherless family, I sought to learn about the life experiences of other women raising their children in planned same-sex fatherless families in Israel, while examining the ways in which "minority stress" manifests itself in their psychological experience and motherhood.

The lesbian Israeli mothers interviewed in this book were 40 middle-class Jewish women aged 26–51. They identified themselves as secular, with the exception of two who defined themselves as Reform and two who were orthodox in the past;

---

1. Hequembourg, 2012; Kranz and Daniluk, 2002; Clarke, 2008

2. The dissertation on which this book is based was written as a PhD thesis at Bar Ilan University under the supervision of Professors Tova Hartman and Rachel Ben-Ari from the Gender Studies Program, Interdisciplinary Studies Unit, and was approved on February 27, 2017.

most of the women had a university degree and live in the socio-economically sturdy center of the country. All participants were biological and/or non-biological mothers raising children with a female partner in a planned (primary) same-sex fatherless family with children between the ages of six months and 19 years. In all cases, the children were conceived via anonymous sperm donation, except for two where the child was adopted from abroad.

The research tools were in-depth semi-structured narrative interviews.[3] The interview data was evaluated according to two methods of analysis: 1) "The Listening Guide: A voice-centered relational method,"[4] and 2) "Mechanisms of selection in claiming narrative identities: A model for interpreting narratives."[5]

Analysis of the interviews showed that the participants were largely preoccupied with constructing a public-representative self-portrait, a representative version of themselves intended for the "world at large," in which they describe themselves as normal, respectable women and ideal mothers. The construction of normality and respectability in the public-representative self-portrait was achieved through relating to the maternal ideal as was formed in Western patriarchal culture (O'Reilly, 2004, 2008), through a complex dialogue of imitation, expansion and resistance. In fact, these women formed their normality and their self-value through two primary strategies: a. demonstrating obedience to the patriarchal maternal ideal, while highlighting the similarities between them and mothers in heterosexual families; and b. negotiating the patriarchal maternal ideal, differentiating themselves from mothers in heterosexual families,

---

3. Zellermeyer, 2010 [Hebrew]; Tuval-Mashiach and Spector-Mersel, 2010 - Rosenthal, 1993.

4. Gilligan and Eddy, 2017; Gilligan et al., 2003.

5. Spector-Mersel, 2011.

and highlighting the unique strengths and advantages of lesbian relationships and motherhood.

However, the "public-representative self-portrait" presented a partial and selective aspect of the narrators' identities.[6] Alongside the dominant voices a "complementary self-portrait" was revealed from which other voices have emerged that were silenced or partially or marginally expressed, in the representative self-presentation. These voices chronicled hardships, stressors, fears and challenges faced by the narrators and their children.

Internal sources of stress, described by the narrators, include:

Vigilance; information management and standing guard in the face of a hostile world; pressure to be an exemplary model of normality and excellence ("the burden of proof"); trial and error; biological inequity and internalized homophobia in the couple's relationship; concerns about the effects of sexual orientation and fatherlessness, and the pressure to raise children with normative sexual and gender identities; the increased stress experienced by children ("affiliate stigma") and challenges of dialogue with them.

External sources of stress reported by the narrators include:

Institutionalized discrimination about same-sex partnerships and parenting, social and economic disadvantages, as well as coping with incidents of rejection, violence and discrimination, inflicted by both families of origin and the medical, educational and social environment.

The life stories described in this book illuminate the life experiences of first-generation women in planned same-sex fatherless families in Israel, as a multidimensional and complex experience, emphasizing the impact of the historic pioneering position and unique socio-cultural contextual conditions in constructing their identity. The "burden of proof," that is, the

---

6. From here on, the study participants will be referred to as "the narrators."

pressure of the narrators to "prove" to themselves and to the heterosexual society that they are normal, women of value and worthy mothers, was the basis for generating a public-representative self-portrait, while at the same time being one of the most significant stressors in their "minority stress" experience.

The oppression and suffering experienced by lesbian families are mostly not acknowledged, nor understood and recognized in the heterosexual society. In this sense, this book contributes to enriching knowledge on the relationship between social stigma and the well-being of minority groups, as well as raising awareness as to the amplified stress experienced by women in planned same-sex families and their children, with all the aspects, meanings and implications involved.

The book ends with outlining the conclusions, principles of action and practical suggestions for legislators, decision and policy makers, as well as for educators and therapists. These could lay down the foundation for interventions at institutional and structural levels, for training experts in the education, health and welfare systems, and developing targeted educational and therapeutic programs. Such interventions and programs could significantly improve the quality of life and physical and mental well-being of LGBTQ people and their families, contributing to a more worthy, equitable and just society.

Chapter 1

LESBIANISM

*Between sexual deviance and
alternative cultural identity*

Lesbianism – Between a personal pathology and revolutionary cultural category

Foucault (1998) was among the most prominent thinkers who argued that sexuality is not a natural characteristic of human life, but a construct whose origins are historical, social and cultural – rather than biological. Butler (2003, 2007) extended this idea when she described gender as a discourse mechanism that itself produces the purported biological reality of the gender binary system (man/woman) and heterosexual attraction, for the purpose of regulating sexuality within the framework of reproduction.

A historical review shows that it was the three major monotheistic religions (Judaism, Christianity, and Islam) that defined sexual activity between members of the same sex, especially sodomy, as a sin and moral abomination, and imposed severe prohibitions and punishments on its enactors. Yet, these sexual practices were not considered components of identity.

In the late 19th and early 20th centuries, the religious and moralistic discourse was replaced by a medical-psychiatric one. The psychiatric discourse regarded same-sex attraction as a mental pathology or sexual perversion resulting in an **identity** or different type of human being: The "homosexual" vs. the "heterosexual."[7] The psychiatric discourse on deviance was largely based on the psychoanalytic theory of Sigmund Freud (2002), who, though acknowledged the inherent bisexuality in humans, described same-sex attraction as a failure in normal psychosexual development. This discourse contributed anew to the establishment of heterosexuality as a cultural norm, and to reinforcing social mechanisms of control and to the oversight of same-sex behavior, its labeling and exclusion (Ziv, 2007).

The belief in the moral superiority of institutions and practices related to heterosexuality is commonly referred to as **heterosexism**. Heterosexism functions as an ideological system that denies, degrades, and stigmatizes any non-heterosexual form of behavior and identity. The term **homophobia** is used to characterize heterosexuals' feelings of horror, hostility, and revulsion toward homosexuals, as well as the self-hatred of homosexuals themselves.[8]

Compulsory heterosexuality and aversion to homosexuality are manifested in two main ways:

1. Structurally and institutionally – through institutional practices that work against them, such as outlawing and penalizing sexual conduct between same-sex individuals; discriminatory laws that attempt to deny gays and lesbians access to reproductive technologies and foster care rights, surrogacy and adoption; lack of legal recognition of same-sex relationships and non-biological same-sex parenting, and so on.

2. Individually and interpersonally, such as experiences of ignoring and silencing, or alternatively, harassment and bullying,

---

7. Foucault, 1998 [Hebrew]; Halperin, 1993.

8. Meyer, 1995, 2003; Ben-Ari, 2001a.

incitement and hatred, incidents of violence and "hate crimes." (Meyer, 2003)

The gay liberation movement arose in the early 1970s in North America and Western Europe against the backdrop of routine police raids and harassment in gay and lesbian entertainment venues in the United States. The movement was a proud declaration (affirmation) of gay and lesbian identity, amidst an oppressive society, and attempted to undermine existing power structures and present a moral alternative to the dominant culture (Gross and Ziv, 2003). At the same time, groundbreaking studies by Kinsey, Hooker, and others, became popular. That proved that same-sex sexual orientation is more prevalent in the population than previously thought, and that homosexuality is not a pathological behavior but a normal variant on the continuum of human sexual behavior.[9] As these developments were occurring, homosexuality was excluded from the American Psychiatric Association's Diagnostic and Statistical Manual (DSM-III) in 1973. This marked the first step in gaining social recognition of gay and lesbian identity and legitimization of same-sex lifestyles.

The development of lesbian identity took place partly separately from its male counterpart, and partly in parallel. In the early 1970s, many lesbians did not find their home in the male-oriented gay liberation movement and opted for the feminist movement. Two of the most prominent representatives of lesbian feminism are Adrienne Rich and Monique Wittig. Rich (2006) defined **compulsory heterosexuality** as the fundamental institution of male oppression. She indicated the variety of coercive and indoctrinating measures imposed on women, to guide them to heterosexuality – from sex trafficking of women, to pay discrimination, to romantic ideology – and argued that if heterosexuality was indeed the natural inclination of

---

9. Luz and Avni, 2000 [Hebrew]; Ben-Ari, 2001b.

most women, there would be no need for such constraints and reinforcements. According to her, women in our society do not have the option of choosing a lesbian or heterosexual "sexual preference." She therefore proposed to redefine lesbianism as a continuum of **women-identified experiences with women** (Baum, 2006; Ziv, 2007). Wittig (2003) analyzed the gender categories of male/female as structural parallels of master/slave, and perceived them as an ideological condition for heterosexuality to exist as an institution that facilitates the exploitation of women. Wittig saw lesbianism as an **act of rebellion against the patriarchy**, since lesbians do not live in subordinate and dependent relationships with men, the same relationships that constitutively establishes women as women. From her point of view, lesbianism is the only social form of existence in which women can be free.

Following the AIDS epidemic of the 1980s, cooperation between lesbians and gays returned, and the radical revolutionary trend was replaced by a more conservative one that aspires to recognition and assimilation. From the 1990s onwards, the struggle of major gay and lesbian organizations has been focused on cultural and institutional recognition of same-sex partnerships and same-sex parenting.[10]

Indeed, the last three decades have seen significant changes in the social conditions of LGBTQ in different parts of the world. More and more countries are demonstrating a more inclusive and accepting attitude towards sexual and gender minorities (Meyer, 2016). A survey that analyzed more than 325 opinion polls conducted in the United States between 1977 and 2014, showed a significant increase in public support for same-sex marriage and adoption rights for same-sex couples (Flores, 2014). In 2011, the United Nations (UN) Human Rights Council

---

10. Amir, 2008 [Hebrew]; Gross and Ziv, 2003 [Hebrew].

passed the first resolution recognizing LGBTQ rights, and called on all countries to apply legal protections for sexual and gender minorities.[11]

Since the 2000s, there has been an increase in the number of countries in which recognition of marriage and other legal arrangements for same-sex partnerships is being discussed. As of 2024, same-sex marriage is legal and recognized, by law or case law, in 36 countries around the world: Andorra, Argentina, Australia, Austria, Belgium, Brazil, Canada, Chile, Columbia, Costa Rica, Cuba, Denmark, Ecuador, Estonia, Finland, France, Germany, Greece, Iceland, Ireland, Luxembourg, Malta, Mexico, the Netherlands, New Zealand, Norway, Portugal Slovenia, South Africa, Spain, Sweden, Switzerland, Taiwan, the United Kingdom, the United States, and Uruguay. (Wikipedia, 2024)

Along with same-sex partnerships, same-sex parenting is gaining increased social and institutional recognition.[12] Same-sex couples are allowed to adopt children in the Netherlands, Sweden, Spain, the United Kingdom, Belgium, Iceland, Norway, Denmark, Andorra, Uruguay, Argentina, Brazil, and South Africa, as well as in some countries in Canada, the United States, Mexico, and Australia. One spouse can apply for adoption or become a guardian for the biological or adopted child of the other spouse in Germany, Finland, Greenland and Israel, as well as in some countries in Canada, the United States and Australia.

There is no law in Israel permitting same-sex marriage because the only authority to marry is vested in the rabbinical courts, which operate according to conservative streams that do not recognize such unions. Same-sex couples can be considered "common-law couples" and thus obtain some of the rights afforded to married couples. Same-sex couples in Israel who

---

11. Human rights, sexual orientation and gender identity, 2011.

12. Masci, et al. 2019; Gates, 2015.

wish to formalize their relationship and clarify their status as "common-law couples" and function as a family unit, have several options: They can conclude a legal agreement between them that defines their relationship; conduct wedding-like ceremonies; and even get married in another country that permits such marriages. In the latter case, they will be registered as married in the marriage registry and on their identification cards, even though it has not been decided whether their marriage is indeed valid in Israel (Ben David, 2009). As for same-sex parenting in Israel, one spouse may apply for an adoption order, a parenting order, or guardianship of his/her spouse's biological or adopted child. Israel's legal recognition of non-biological parenting is not based on recognition of same-sex families in principle, but of "personal circumstances." (Triger, 2006).

The mainstream focus of LGBTQ organizations on the project of affirming LGBTQ identities and gaining equal rights similar to the heterosexual society, has produced a backlash in the form of queer theory. Queer theory (Jagose, 1996) proposes to replace oppressive and restrictive notions of identity such as "gay" and "lesbian" with the term "queer," as an anti-identity and gender-neutral identity category, and expresses opposition to the notion of "assimilation" and the desire for "normality." However, feminist critics warn against erasing the lesbian identity within the queer identity, as well as the disappearance of the gender hierarchy under the guise of transcending gender divisions (Gross and Ziv, 2003).

Lesbianism in Israel – Sappho in the Holy Land

In Israel, marital law is based on the Orthodox Jewish religion, which does not permit same-sex marriage, and does not recognize the same-sex family as a legitimate form. However, since the 1990s, as the gay and lesbian communities joined together to fight for equal rights, significant legal developments have been achieved, on the status of same-sex couples and families in Israel. For example, in 1994, the Supreme Court recognized the status of same-sex couples for the first time; and in 2005, the Supreme Court ruled that a lesbian couple can adopt each other's offspring. There have been more significant breakthroughs when the Supreme Court demanded that same-sex couples, who wed in a civil marriage in Canada, be registered as married couples in the population registry of the State of Israel (Meir, 2008); the Ministry of Interior began issuing appropriate identification cards for children of same-sex couples (Lior, 2014); same-sex couples can obtain parental recognition through an expedited "parenting order" instead of an adoption order (Avni, 2015); and starting from 2022, same-sex couples were able to exercise their right to be parents through surrogacy and adoption (Peleg, 2022; Bendel, 2023). At the same time, the LGBTQ community is continuing its fight for the right of same-sex couples to marry in Israel.[13]

There is a plethora of evidence regarding the divided attitudes in Israeli society toward the phenomenon of homosexuality: Alongside a growing number of men and women, including esteemed artists and cultural icons, who publicly declare their sexual orientation, the development of local same-sex communities, and the procession of gay pride parades in various cities in Israel, homosexuals in Israel continue to suffer from stigmas and discrimination, hate speech and incitement, and extreme acts of violence – some of which have claimed physical and mental victims, such as the stabbing attacks of Jerusalem Gay Pride Parade marchers in 2006 and 2015, and the Tel Aviv LGBTQ Youth Center shooting in 2009.[14]

---

13. Lior, 2015 [Hebrew].
14. Lees and Scope, 2016 [Hebrew]; Kushrek, 2010 [Hebrew].

In recent years, homosexuality has also been a topic of discussion among the Orthodox Jewish community in Israel, sparking up a storm and controversy. Thus, while there is hate speech and incitement by some more conservative rabbis and demonstrations by some of the religious public against holding gay pride parades in Jerusalem, more moderate rabbis are calling for dialogues with religious LGBTQ organizations, and for the inclusion of LGBTQ individuals in religious communities.[15]

Israeli feminist thinkers and researchers, Kadish (2005) and Shadmi (2007, 2005) argue that a Jewish lesbian woman in Israel, whose "life partner" is not a man, and who is not a member of the patriarchal nuclear family, poses a threat to heteronormative Israeli ideology and is therefore subject to silencing and oppression. However, she does not serve as the "ultimate other," since that position is reserved for Palestinians. The fact that Jewish lesbian women in Israel are one step ahead or aren't the "ultimate other ," allows them to maneuverability and a certain degree of acceptance, even though their acceptance remains borderline.

---

15. Ettinger, 2010, 2016 [Hebrew]; Ilani, 2009 [Hebrew]; Fridson, et al., 2019 [Hebrew]; Kaizer, 2010 [Hebrew].

Chapter 2

LESBIAN MOTHERHOOD

'Can two walk together, except they be agreed?'

The invention of modern motherhood

The modern form of motherhood, as we know it today, developed against the backdrop of the Industrial Revolution at the end of the 18th century. Then production moved from the home to capitalist industry to form a division of labor in which men dominated the public domains of economics and politics and women and children inherited the domestic and private domains. Influenced by the belief that every woman wants to and should be a mother, and that every child needs his mother, women took on the role of physical, mental, and emotional caretakers of children, almost exclusively (Friedman, 2007).

Throughout most of the 20th century, an ideology of the **"ideal mother"** developed in the Western World (O'Reilley, 2004, 2008). The "ideal mother" was expected to meet all her child's needs immediately and at all times. She was also expected to provide independent, unconditional love without portraying any negative or ambivalent emotions.[16] Prominent theorists such as Freud, Bowlby, Klein, and others, reinforced that ideology by placing onus for the child's development and mental

---

16. DiQuinzio, 1999; Hequembourg, 2012; Thurer, 1994.

health on the mother. Mothers were accused of the opposite – of not providing enough love or loving too much, emotional detachment or manipulation, being too controlling, overprotective, or criminally negligent. Even theories that attempted to challenge the myth of the ideal mother, such as Winnicott's "good enough mother" theory (Winnicott, 1973), have become impossible to realize (Friedman, 2007).

The attitude of feminist theories toward the issue of motherhood is quite complex, spanning extreme edges: Alongside feminist thinkers such as Simone de Beauvoir, Shulamit Firestone, and Rich, who protested the assumption that every woman was "naturally" destined to be a mother, and viewed the female body and maternal role as woman's primary source of oppression, other feminist theorists, such as Dinnerstein and O'Brien, perceived motherhood as woman's primary source of power (Friedman, 2007).

Rich (2021) made an important distinction between motherhood as a social institution, and motherhood as a personal experience, while Chodoro (2007, 1999) and Gilligan (1990) pointed out how the work of parenting, which is mostly assigned to women, reproduces the different psychological and interpersonal development of men and women, which results in an unequal gender division of roles in society, while paying particular attention to mother-daughter relationships.

Thinkers, who followed in the footsteps of Chodoro and Gilligan, emphasized the influence of cultural contexts and social power relations on the work of motherhood. Hartman (2002) noted that mothers serve as agents of socialization within a culture, or, more precisely, within a number of cultures, which marginalize women (to one degree or another); accordingly, they are forced to be in constant negotiation with the conventions, regulations, and cultural prohibitions imposed on women and girls, moving along a continuum of silencing, protecting, confrontation, and initiation. Under conditions of a hierarchical society, in which women suffer from gender oppression, and sometimes oppression based on socioeconomic status, race, ethnicity, sexual orientation, or religious affinity, maternal thinking can be inauthentic and lead to reacting in obedience of dominant values, at the expense of cultivating the children's personal development and growth in other directions.[17]

Following up on the theoretical literature's treatment of motherhood reveals that, at least at the outset, both psychoanalytic and feminist theories regard the mother as an **object** – that is, as someone whose being is summarized by her giving and being devoted to the needs of her children, and erased her as a person with needs and desires of her own (Palgi-Hecker, 2005). However, recent decades, have seen a slow and gradual transition in the psychoanalytic world and in feminist thinking from a pal-centric and paternal position to a **maternal** position, which offers more space to the subjective experiences of the mother and is based on principles of compassion, protection, and inclusion (Peroni, 2009).[18]

Mothers in Israel – 'Bearers of the Collective' in 'The Land of Obligatory Motherhood'

The sociologist Fogel-Bizhawi (1999) argued that while in most Western countries, the conventional nuclear family (i.e., a family consisting of a father who is the primary breadwinner and a mother who works part-time or is a housewife, who raise their biological children under one roof) is losing its centrality. Yet, in Israel the centrality of the normative nuclear family is

---

17. Hartman, 2002; Hill Collins, 1994; Ruddick, 1989, 2005.

18. Examples of this transition can be found, in the works of Lieblich (2003, 2009) [Hebrew], Ben-Ari and Livni (2006) [Hebrew],and Ben-Ari and Weinberg (2007) [Hebrew].

preserved. According to her, postmodern processes of individualization and democratization in the family institution are the fate of Israeli families from a narrow social stratum, rather than of Israeli society as a whole.

Indeed, a comparison between Israel and other developed countries reveals that Israel is the fertility champion, with a birth rate of about three children per woman, compared to 1.4 in northern and western Europe, and 1.9 in the United States. In addition, divorce rates in Israel are relatively low (although increasing), only 15 percent of births result in registered abortions, and unmarried mothers give birth to less than one percent of all babies (Remennick, 2000).

The enormous importance given to mothers (especially, biological motherhood) and to family hood in the State of Israel is the result of unique cultural and historical factors: Religious Jewish heritage, in which "be fruitful and multiply" is one of the most important commandments; the need to grow the Jewish nation after much of it was destroyed in the Holocaust in Europe; the social obligation to "make soldiers for the Israel Defense Forces" amidst the precarious security situation in Israel; demographic competition with Arab neighbors; everyday culture being centered on children, and so on.[19]

In the Israeli patriarchy, where women are inferior citizens to men, motherhood is their ticket to participating in the national collective. A woman who is not a mother is not merely a "non-woman ," that is, not only is her feminine identity being questioned, but also her right to public existence and to having a social voice.[20]

---

19. Lieblich, 2009 [Hebrew]; Remennick, 2000.
20. Berkowitz; 1999 [Hebrew]; Friedman; 2007 [Hebrew], Zidkiyahu; 2004 [Hebrew].

Lesbian Motherhood in Israel

Regarding the importance and centrality of the family unit, Israeli society constitutes a unique social and cultural context, compared to other Western countries. The mainstream LGBTQ community doesn't challenge conservative social institutions such as marriage and the nuclear family; on the contrary, it fights for the right to participate in them. Israeli researchers Ben-Ari and Efrat (2002), who interviewed Israeli lesbian adolescents on "coming out of the closet," found that all the interviewees expressed their desire to one day become mothers. In fact, they all imagined their adult lives as lesbians in a "traditional" family structure, involving two parents and children, not one imagined herself as a single mother. Moreover, in many cases, adult lesbian women in Israel are not happy with the problematic status of "non-biological mother ," and aspire to become mothers of biological children, with all the legal and social privileges that this status implies (Ben-Ari and Livni, 2006). According to the researchers, lesbian mothers in Israel struggle with a dialectic between experiencing marginalization and diversity on account of their being lesbian, and conformism and commitment to familyhood that is so deeply rooted in Israeli culture. For them, the transition to motherhood marks their joining mainstream society and the social acceptance of themselves and their families.

In contrast to their peers in the Western World,[21] lesbian women in Israel, at various stages of parenthood, emphasized that they enjoy encouragement and support from LGBTQ friends and community to have and raise children.[22] This encouragement and support is expressed in a "family-oriented" daily life of gay and lesbian community members in Israel. It includes groups for LGBTQ parents and pre-parenting groups, activities for

---

21. DeMino, et al., 2007; Jordan, 2009.

22. Efrat, 1999 [Hebrew]; Lieblich, 2009 [Hebrew]; Zidkiyahu; 2004 [Hebrew], Ben-Ari and Livni 2006.

children in the community, annual conferences on "Rainbow Families," and more. In fact, it wouldn't be an exaggeration to claim that in recent years, the same-sex community in Israel has not only encouraged, but also pressured lesbian and gay individuals to become parents. A lesbian woman in Israel who doesn't want to be a mother is considered a "strange bird ," even among most of her gay and lesbian friends (Davidov, 2011).

The development of the 'lesbian mother' category – the transition from 'not a woman' to 'model mother'

Tracking the evolving formation of the 'lesbian mother' category over 100 years of psychological research (Clarke, 2008) reveals five different eras:

- **Late 19th century and early 20th century – the masculine lesbian:** At the beginning of the 20th century, early sexologists described lesbians as masculine women, infertile and unfit to raise healthy children and, accordingly, an outsider to marriage, family, and motherhood. In other words, the terms "lesbian" and "motherhood" were considered antonyms.
- **Mid-20th century – the underdeveloped lesbian:** In 1952, psychoanalytically-trained psychiatrists classified homosexuality as a "sexual perversion," and lesbians were defined as women with underdeveloped, infantile sexuality, who did not express a "natural" female desire for marriage and motherhood, feared pregnancy and childbirth, and were not mature enough to raise children. Opinions about "curing" lesbians by "transforming" them into heterosexual were divided, fearing that they would marry and bear "damaged" children like they are.
- **1970s – emergence of the (problematic) category of 'lesbian mother':** With the outbreak of the second wave of feminism, and the removal of homosexuality from the DSMIII in

1973, more and more women, who had children in heterosexual family units, began to openly identifying themselves as lesbians. However, many of these mothers have found themselves fighting for custody in courtrooms (and often losing) as a result of the prejudice that lesbians were unfit to parent and negatively affect their children's psychosexual development.

- **1980s – 'The 'as-good-as-(a heterosexual) lesbian mother' vs. the 'bad lesbian mother':** During the 1980s, most researchers compared lesbian mothers and their children to heterosexual mothers and their children. The studies found no significant differences between the two groups in terms of the mothers' parental competence and their children's development.

  However, this comparison led to a distinction between two opposing images of the "lesbian mother": The "as-good-as-(a heterosexual)-lesbian-mother" vs. the "bad lesbian mother." "Good lesbian mothers" were defined as those who keep their sexuality private, separate from and subject to their motherhood. In order to prove their parental competence and gain custody of their children, judges often required them to separate from their spouses, to "downplay" their lesbianism, and not engage in political activism. In contrast, "bad lesbian mothers" were defined as selfish, combative, man-hating, and "missionary" about their identity, and they almost always lost custody of their children.

- **1990s and 2000s – the 'new' lesbian parent reinvents the family:** The 1990s and 2000s saw a rapid rise in the number of lesbian and gay individuals choosing to raise children in planned family units – through artificial insemination of a known or anonymous donor, adoption, and a variety of co-parenting arrangements. Researchers and therapists who compared planned lesbian families to heterosexual families on variables such as role division in the home, childcare, and parent-child relationships, came up with a new narrative of "the better-than-(heterosexual families) lesbian family." Some even argued that the lesbian family is at the forefront of "postmodern families" as it is "reinventing the family."

British researchers Clarke and Kitzinger[23] analyzed the content of talk shows, documentaries, and newspaper articles, as well as focus groups and interviews with same-sex parents in England, to examine how gay and lesbian families have been portrayed in the public sphere in recent years. They found that the most prevalent discourse is the "normalizing" one, which emphasizes the similarities between gay and lesbian families and heterosexual families, and denies or downplays the importance of any (sexual) differences. According to the researchers, the most prevalent "normalization strategies" are:

- **'I am not a gay/lesbian parent' (just a parent who also happens to be same-sex)** – by rejecting the category of "gay/lesbian parent," same-sex parents emphasize their similarity and "normality ," and challenge the assumption that they are fundamentally different from heterosexual parents (due to their sexuality).
- **'We're just like the family next door'** – gay and lesbian parents use this argument to illustrate the mundaneness and banality of their daily lives. The argument attempts to provide an answer to hostile rhetoric that portrays the supposedly glorious and promiscuous 'LGBTQ lifestyle' as the antithesis of stable and moral family values.
- **'Love makes a family'** – the most common strategy used to protect LGBTQ parents, emphasizes the critical importance of the quality of relationships, especially love, care, and security

---

23. Clarke, 2002; Clarke and Kitzinger, 2004.

in defining a family and creating a healthy and functioning family unit. Arguments about love correspond directly with common heterosexist assumptions that define a "family" according to heterosexual structure and blood ties between parents and children.

- **'God created Adam and Steve'** – This strategy of resistance attempts to address the perception that gay and lesbian parenting is a religious and moral sin. Proponents of same-sex parenting argue that God created lesbian and gay people, that God is love, and that the Bible supports their position.

- **'Children as proof'** – children of lesbian and gay spouses are usually invited to talk shows to dispel concerns about the negative psychological impact of same-sex parenting and prove that they are like other children, healthy and "normal" (i.e. heterosexual).

- **'The benefits of growing up in a gay or lesbian family'** – groups that advocate same-sex parenting tend to emphasize two main benefits for such children: Being planned, chosen, and wanted, and their opportunity to develop understanding and openness about diversity.

Confirmation of the "normalization discourse" of LGBTQ families in academic and public domains can be found in other articles[24] that reviewed dozens of studies comparing lesbian families to heterosexual ones, and emphasize the similarities between the two family types regarding parental functioning and child adjustment. Studies yielded no significant differences between adolescents and young adults raised in lesbian families, and those raised in heterosexual ones, regarding the development of gender identity and sexual orientation.[25]

---

24. Patterson, 1995 [Hebrew]; Patterson, 1992; Bos, et al., 2004.

25. Gartrell, et al., 2011; Golombok and Badger, 2010; Tasker and Golombok, 1995.

The benefits of growing up in a same-sex family tend to also be emphasized in academic and public discourse. Many studies investigating the division of roles and parental functioning in lesbian family units, have shown that mothers in same-sex families were characterized by a shared decision-making style and a more equal and flexible division of roles, compared to heterosexual couples.[26] Other researchers have indicated that children, adolescents, and young adults who were raised in lesbian families, have higher self-esteem, better social skills, display higher academic achievements, and are less likely to engage in aggressive and antisocial behavior than children, adolescents, and young adults who were raised in heterosexual families.[27]

Similarly, anyone perusing articles published in print or electronically in Israel in recent years, will likely encounter articles highlighting similarities between the achievements of children growing up in families headed by two mothers or two fathers, and those of children growing up in families headed by a father and a mother. Moreover, studies that have found differences, will generally point to a clear advantage in favor of children of same-sex parents in a variety of areas, including self-confidence, sociability, academic achievements, openness, and acceptance of differences.[28]

In fact, the public gradually finds itself exposed to a "new breed" of lesbian and gay people. The familiar stereotypes and representations of the lonely and neglected masculine lesbian and the glorious and ridiculed feminine gay, are now being replaced by representations of polite and decent women and men, from middle class and above, raising healthy and well-groomed

26. Or, 2000 [Hebrew]; Patterson, 1992; Bos, et al., 2005.

27. Schechter, 2009 [Hebrew]; Golombok and Badger, 2010; Van Gartrell and Bos, 2010; Gelderen, et al., 2012.

28. Gewirtz, 2010 [Hebrew]; Glazer, 2017 [Hebrew]; Heifetz-Schwartz, 2010 [Hebrew]; Levy, 2010 [Hebrew]; Haaretz Service, 2009 [Hebrew].

children. At the same time, Clarke points out the dangers inherent in normalizing and idealizing same-sex parents, and turning them into symbols and models of equal relationships and beneficial parenting. She argues that such glorification may re-label them as "inhuman," once again silencing their unique difficulties and challenges, and give renewed validity to heteronormative assumptions by which they are measured and judged (Clarke, 2008).

Dismantling the 'necessary father' myth

Planned lesbian fatherless families are a highly charged and controversial family model, especially in a society that identifies the nuclear family with a heterosexual system, one that is considered essential to establishing the mental health and sexual identity of the child. According to the psychoanalysis of Freud and Lacan, the mother-father-child trinity is at the heart of the Oedipus complex, and its solution drives the child's transition from a pre-social position to one that facilitates language acquisition and understanding of the law; The Oedipus complex is also the process by which a person's feminine and masculine identity is formed, and the nature of their sexual desire is determined (Rosemary, 2010).

Over the last two decades, the patriarchal nuclear family in the United States seems to have been nostalgically idealized in particular. Neoconservative clergy, policymakers, and social scientists tend to attribute many of the problems facing the American society (such as child poverty, social violence, teenage pregnancy, and low scholastic achievements) to the absence of fathers in children's lives (Silverstein and Auerbach, 1999).

Researchers and professionals[29] followed the development of children growing up in different family constellations to examine these claims and concluded that children benefit from stable, consistent, loving, and conflict-free arrangements, regardless of the gender of the parents or the biological relation of the parent to the child. According to them, at the basis of the "fear of fatherlessness" lie political and social interests, aimed at restoring fathers to positions of power and control in their families, at a time when the hegemony of the patriarchal nuclear family is losing its power and validity.

Cultural feminists, such as Benjamin, Chodoro, and Gilligan, who reexamined the question: "What is a legitimate family structure?" advocate a broader definition for the family position of "mother" and the family position of "father ," such that could be occupied by any of the two genders. Yet, the cultural scholar Butler, detaches herself from a notable tradition of psychoanalytic feminism when she defies the very assumption that there must be a father's place and a mother's place, and that someone is supposed to hold these titles, otherwise they will remain empty and cause deprivation and defect (Rosemary, 2010). In her recent books, Butler (2001, 2010) calls for dismantling the self-evident status of the nuclear family, and expanding the horizon to include more forms of human organizations, unbound by the scales of masculine/feminine and paternal/maternal.

A review of the development of the sociocultural discourse on parenting in general and same-sex parenting in particular, reveals normalization and humanization processes in the construction of the "lesbian mother" category. At the same time, the heteronormative assumption regarding the necessity of a man/father in every family, is subject to processes of appeal and dissolution.

---

29. MacCallum and Golombok, 2004; Perlesz, 2005; Schnitzer, 1998; Silverstein and Auerbach, 1999.

Chapter 3

THE HYBRID ZONE

Negotiating identity and belonging,
and managing stigma

Identity in the 'hybrid zone'

Today's motherhood and new familyhood allow lesbian women to reconnect with the mainstream of heterosexual society and enjoy recognition, acceptance and social appreciation. However, a closer reading of descriptions of lesbian mothers from around the Western world, gives the impression that this experience is more multifaceted and complex. Mann (2007), for example, used the metaphor of fragmentation to describe mixed feelings of belonging, confusion, and self-alienation from the moment she became a lesbian mother. Similarly, the British theorist Gabb (2004) used the term "dislocation" when referring to her experience as a lesbian mother at a gay pride parade in London; from her perspective, lesbian mothers are trapped in a constant state of oscillation, deprived of any stable identity.

While Mann mourns the loss of what she calls "lesbian difference," which she describes as a site of vitality and resistance, Gabb believes that lesbian families don't lose their difference and power of resistance, expressing it by "disrupting" common heterosexual narratives of gender, reproduction, and procreation roles. Gabb's claim is reinforced by the ideas of the cultural scholar Butler (2001, 2007, 2010). Butler emphasized the productive function in addition to the subversive one of alternative kinship systems. In her opinion, since families with two mothers constitute an unauthorized, inaccurate repetition of the same norms and hearsay practices that constitute the "family" identity category, they not only challenge the "naturalness" of the category, but also construct new types of subjectivity and new social configurations.

The transition from a marginal, abnormal, and despised identity ("lesbian") to a central, "normal" and valued identity ("mother") is not unique to lesbian women raising children. Similar processes were observed among other minority groups, which underwent processes of re-initiation, "normalization, "acculturation," or "whitening." These groups include black men and women who reached positions of power in the United States, refugees who emigrated from colonies, such as India and Africa, to empires of origin – England and France, Mizrahi women in Israel who studied in schools of Ashkenazi elites and became more "Ashkenazic," and so on. Fanon (2008), a black psychiatrist who was born in a French colony, lived in France for several years, and ultimately fought in the Algerian War against the French, using the image "black skin, white masks" to describe the experience of duplicity and conflict felt by a black man subjected to a re-initiation of white colonial rule, trying to be different from those who are "different" in order to resemble the white ruler.

Bhabha (1990, 1994), who studied power relations between minority and dominant cultures in postcolonial theories, coined the terms "hybridity" and "the third space" to describe a space for negotiation and translation of cultural identities during periods of historical transformation. The poet and cultural theorist Anzaldúa (2012) used the term "borderlands" to redefine "identity," not as belonging to a specific group with distinct characteristicsח racial, ethnic, sexual, or national, but rather as a hybrid zone, a crossroads of cultures, a space of contradictions, in which new consciousnesses and new definitions of culture and belonging are formed:

> *As a mestiza I have no country, my homeland cast me out; yet all countries are mine because I am every woman's sister or potential lover. (As a lesbian I have no race, my own people disclaim me; but I am all races because there is the queer of me in all races.) I am cultureless because, as a feminist, I challenge the collective cultural/religious male- derived beliefs of Indo-Hispanic and Anglos; yet I am cultured because I am participating in the creation of yet another culture, a new story to explain the world and our participation in it, a new value system with images and symbols that connect us to each other and to the planet.* (Anzaldúa, 2012: 363)

The new and unique consciousness of people from minority groups, who are gaining a foothold in the institutions of the ruling social elite, can also be gleaned from black and Eastern feminists. The black feminist Patricia Hill Collins (1991) emphasized that the position of African-American women in the American political economy, especially their employment in housework and childcare in the homes of white elites, allowed them to develop a unique perspective, which she calls the "outsider within" phenomenon. From that vantage point, it is possible to learn, for example, about the contradictions between the declared ideologies of the dominant group and its actual actions.

Similarly, the Mizrahi Israeli feminist Dahan-Caleb (2000) described the "Ashkenization" process in a school in Jerusalem, when she hid her Moroccan origins from her friends and introduced herself as a French girl. She adopted practices of imitating form, language, appearance and disguise, to cloak herself in an Israeli-Ashkenazi visage and hide any Mizrahi "differences." According to her, the "disguise" of being an Ashkenazi girl made the repressed Moroccan girl invisible, but the "repressed girl" refused to disappear and continued to observe what was happening and even yearn for recognition. This unique position of seeing and not being seen, helped her construct a different, mysterious, hidden story, a type of reflection of the revealed story, that responded dialectically to a reality determined by the hegemonic narrator (ibid., p. 199).

In conclusion, the thinkers and researchers who studied processes of "normalization," "re-civilization," and approaching the center among various minority groups, tended to use visual metaphors, such as sight and blindness, presence and absence, marking and transparency, the gaze of the "outsider within," "seeing and not being seen," and metaphors of space and geographical location, such as home and exile, wilderness, border zones, a "third space," and a new territory. In addition, the terms and images used were based on the relationship of a complex dialectic between outlooks and experiences that were perceived as contrary to each other.

Coping with social stigma

The American researcher Meyer (1995, 2003) used the term "minority stress" to describe the increased stress experienced by people of different sexual orientations (gay, lesbian, bisexual, and more) by virtue of belonging to a social category that carries with it a stigma or a negative social label. According to him, the experience of "minority stress" carries with it five prominent aspects among gay and lesbian people: 1) Conditions of external stress, such as the lack of legal recognition of same-sex relationships; 2) Stressful events such as a violent incident; 3) Anticipated stigma, i.e., expecting rejection, violence, and discrimination on homophobic grounds; 4) Concealment of sexual orientation and identity; and 5) Internalized homophobia, i.e., internalizing negative social attitudes towards the self and towards people from sexual minorities, in general.

There is research evidence that a high level of "minority stress" experienced by people with different sexual orientations, measured by each of the different components, tends to be significantly associated with different measures of psychological issues, such as symptoms of anxiety and depression, substance abuse, at-risk behaviors, suicidal thoughts, and various forms of self-harm (Meyer, 1995, 2003). Anticipated stigma predicted psychological distress among gay men to a greater extent than actual negative experiences (Ross, 1985). Internalized homophobia was also associated with difficulties in intimate relationships and sexual functioning.[30]

The issue of experiencing increased stress in the context of lesbian families is confirmed and echoes in a number of quantitative studies in Israel and abroad. Mothers in lesbian families in Israel (couples and singles) received less help from families of origin in terms of information, emotional support, and financial assistance, compared to mothers in heterosexual couple families (Meir, 2008). Young adults who grew up in same-sex families reported more incidents of violence and rejection by peers than young adults who grew up in single heterosexual families in the United States (Tasker and Golombok, 1995).

Cross-cultural research has shown that lesbian mothers, living in the United States, a country where the legal and social rights granted to citizens of different sexual orientations in 2009 were more limited than in Canada, reported a greater number of family concerns around legal status and discrimination, and symptoms of depression, compared to lesbian mothers

---

30. Meyer, 1995, 2003; Shildo, 1994; Williamson, 2000.

living in Canada (Shapiro et al 2009). At the same time, children who grew up in the Netherlands in planned lesbian families were more open about their family structure, experienced less homophobia, and exhibited fewer emotional and behavioral issues than American children (Bos et al. 2008).

And finally, Bos, et al. (2004) examined the relationship between "minority stress" and parenting experiences, coping styles, and child adjustment among mothers in planned same-sex families in the Netherlands. They found that lesbian mothers who faced many events of rejection, experienced a higher degree of parental pressure, tended to defend their parental position more strongly, and described more behavioral issues among their children. A tendency to be defensive and justified by parents was also associated with high levels of anticipated stigma and internalized homophobia. Lesbian mothers in planned families in the United States reported a higher level of stress and anxiety about revealing sexual orientation than childless lesbian women. They tended to use a coping style of selectively disclosing information about their sexual orientation and family differences to protect their children from stigma and violence (DeMino, et al 2007).

This book aims to examine the meaning of the transition of lesbian Jewish women in Israel to motherhood and familyhood: How they construct their identity and level of belonging, what cultural edicts and directives they use to negotiate, and how they interpret their life experiences and motherhood while undergoing this transition. Borrowing from other theories that have examined similar processes of minority groups that have undergone re-initiation or normalization, it is important to learn whether the transition to motherhood and familyhood constitutes for them a "homecoming" from forced exile, imprisons them in a hybrid zone, or allows them to create their own "(new) home."

Special attention is given to the questions: Does the "minority stress" of parents and children in same-sex families fade away and disappear under conditions of normalization, and as they near the social center? and if not, which new forms and expressions does it receive? these questions are consistent with Meyer's (2016) call to examine the impact of positive changes in the social environment on the life experiences and mental well-being of LGBTQ and their families. Listening to the unique difficulties, stressors, and challenges faced by women and children in planned same-sex fatherless families can shed light on these questions.

This new knowledge will make a significant contribution to the understanding of stigma, quality of life, and well-being among parents and children in same-sex families in Israel, as well as in other countries. In addition, it will serve as a basis for proposing an actionable outline for decision makers, policy makers, educators, and therapists.

Chapter 4

LESBIAN MOTHERHOOD
UNDER THE BURDEN OF PROOF
Public-representative Self-Portrait

The narrators in the book painted a public-representative
self-portrait, a representative version of themselves intended for the "wider world," in which they describe themselves as
normal, valuable women and worthy mothers. The construct
of normality and of value and respectability was brought about
through correspondence with the patriarchal maternal ideal and
with dominant meta-narratives in Western society, that define
what good femininity and proper motherhood are, while engaging in a complex dialogue of imitation, expansion, and resistance.

Heterosexism and homophobia largely define who is a "good
wife" and a "proper mother." The "ideal mother," as portrayed
in contemporary media and popular culture, is white, heterosexual, fertile, married, middle-class, physically and mentally
fit, has two children, and is supported by her husband.[31] While
the married heterosexual mother ranks at the top of the "hierarchy of motherhood" as the "most worthy mother," the lesbian
mother ranks at the bottom of the hierarchy as the "least worthy

---

31. O'Reilly, 2004, 2008; DiLapi, 1989.

mother," due to her rejection of male domination, embodied in sexual relations with men and in the presence of a man/father in the family (DiLapi, 1989).

The American researcher O'Reilly (2004, 2008) defined eight 'rules' of **'good' motherhood** as dictated by the **ideal patriarchal mother**:[32] 1. Children can only be properly cared for by their biological mother; 2. This mothering must be provided 24/7; 3. The mother must always put children's needs before her own; 4. Mothers must turn to the experts for instruction; 5. The mother must be fully satisfied, fulfilled, completed, and composed in motherhood; 6. Mothers must lavish excessive amounts of time, energy, and money in the rearing of their children; 7. The mother has full responsibility, but no power with which to mother; 8. Mother work, and more specifically, childrearing, are regarded as personal, private undertakings with no political import.

Women raising children in same-sex fatherless families, do not meet the criteria of a "proper family," as defined in patriarchal and heteronormative culture, in a number of notable aspects: They have a relationship with a woman who is also a co-mother, there is no man/father in the family, and family ties are not based exclusively on biological blood ties. Hetero-sexist cultural beliefs and "anti-lesbian mythologies" tend to cast doubt on the mental health, morality, and parenting skills of lesbian women. A lesbian woman is usually judged as being too selfish, unhealthy, immoral, and childish, to be capable of providing her children with security and stability, physical care and emotional support. She is also perceived as being overly sexual and liable to rape her children. Finally, she is accused of condemning her children to trauma, disgrace, and social ostracism for all of their lives.[33]

---

32. From here on I will use the term "patriarchal maternal ideal," as defined by the researcher Andrea O'Reilly (O'Reilly, 2004; 2008).

33. Hequemberg, 2012; Kranz and Daniluk, 2002.

Furthermore, the hegemony of the nuclear patriarchal family continues to merit the support of clerics and conservative social scientists. The presence of a father in the family is considered essential for the proper psychological and sexual development of children, and necessary for setting boundaries and discipline, supervision, and financial security. The absence of a father figure is seen as potentially damaging to the self-image, gender identity, and sexual orientation of children, especially boys.[34]

An analysis of the narratives' accounts revealed that they used two primary strategies to construct their image as normal women and respectful, worthy mothers, as illustrated and detailed below:

Demonstrating obedience to the ideal patriarchal mother and emphasizing the similarities between them and mothers in heterosexual families.

Negotiating the ideal patriarchal mother, distinguishing themselves from mothers in heterosexual families, and highlighting the unique strengths and advantages of lesbian relationships and motherhood.

The construct of normality and normativity – highlighting similarities to heterosexual mothers

The narrators in this book, the first generation of lesbian women in Israel raising children in planned same-sex fatherless families, portrayed their images, first and foremost, as normal, normative women. The construct of "normality" and "normativity" was based on imitating the "ideal patriarchal mother" (O'Reilly, 2004) and highlighting the similarities between them and mothers in heterosexual families.

---

34. Rozmarin, 2010 [Hebrew]; Silverstein and Auerbach, 1999; Schnitzer, 1998.

The narrators demonstrated how they adhere to the values of the "ideal patriarchal mother ," such as essentialism, availability, optimal care, placing the child at the center, and lack of maternal ambivalence, implement its practices with great success, and even stretch it to new heights of "excellence." These values are consistent with the principles of the maternal ideal, as found in the consciousness of middle-class heterosexual mothers in Israel: 1) Dedicated physical care and emotional support; 2) The principle of presence and availability in children's lives; 3) Providing a significant and central place for the children's needs; 4) Lack of negative feelings towards children (Shayovitz-Gurman, 2009).

The intention behind demonstrating adherence to the rules of the maternal ideal and highlighting similarities between the narrators and mothers in heterosexual families, is to combat "anti-lesbian mythologies" and cultural mechanisms of devaluation that question the mental health, morality, and parental competence of lesbian women.[35] In other words, they make themselves out to be normal, normative women, wishing to (re-)enter the domain of "femininity" and "humanity," from which they were "exiled" when they exposed themselves as lesbians and voluntarily renounced male sexual domination.

Many narrators spoke of their mothers in terms of a natural, fateful, and inevitable fate. Child rearing and childcare are, for them, natural, essential, necessary, and unquestionable practices that have nothing to do with their sexual orientation or the fact that they did or did not give birth to the children. These narratives are consistent with the ideology of "essential motherhood,"[36] which views motherhood as a necessary fulfillment of the natural essence of every woman.

---

35. Hequemberg, 2012; Kranz and Daniluk, 2002; Schnitzer, 1998.
36. DiQuinzio, 1999; Hequembourg, 2012.

The act of naturalizing motherhood by the narrators is done with two main strategies. One strategy is mystification, in other words, defining motherhood in terms of a predestined fate from birth. The second strategy is essentialism, meaning, the portrayal of motherhood as an essential and integral part of a mother's identity, without which they would be incomplete as human beings and women. The use of the mystification strategy has also been observed among other groups of mothers who face social stigma, oppression, and discrimination. For example, single adoptive heterosexual mothers in Israel tended to describe the relationship with their children as a "fateful union," charging it with an emotional quality of mutual and deliberate choice ("a match made in heaven") in order to cope with the double marginalization: Non-biological motherhood and single motherhood (Ben-Ari and Weinberg-Kurnik, 2007).

The concept of motherhood as a fateful vocation from birth can be gleaned from Lily's words. Lily (a biological mother of a 5-year-old and 2.5-year-old in her 30s) described herself as "a woman destined to give birth and be a mother of people." She interpreted the fact that her partner was unable to get pregnant after three years of fertility treatments, while she got pregnant quickly and had relatively easy pregnancies and births, as a "sign from heaven" that she was destined to be the birth mother, and that her partner was destined to be the co-mother in raising the children:

When we first started trying to expand the family to include children, Ella [her partner A.P.] began trying to conceive first. Oh, the reason we chose to begin with her... It's just a matter of biology. We're five years apart – she's older than me, so it was obvious that she'd start trying first. It didn't work out with her. She spent nearly 3 years in fertility treatments that led to no results, not even a miscarriage. And then we moved on to me... It turns out that I must have been destined to have a baby. Not only did I get pregnant very quickly, the pregnancy itself was easy for me, including the births. So we decided that I would give birth to the kids and that she would raise them. I am simply a mother! I was destined, fated to give birth and be people's mother! And she was simply born to be the raising mother!

Heidi (a non-biological mother to a 10-year-old boy and 8-year-old girl in her late 40s) claimed that she was not predestined to give birth and hence did not miss out on the birthing experience, but that she was born to be the mother of her non-biological children. The phrase "was born to" was repeated four times. Word repetition serves to refine the primary message (the end point – EP) in asserting a narrative identity. Refinement makes it possible to give prominence to some of the experiences and events, by thickening or exaggerating parts of the story that promote the central message (Spector-Mersel, -2011):

My experience with the transition to motherhood was easy, as though I was born to do it. Yes, I truly was destined for it. For me, being pregnant was the most magical thing in the world. It was as though I was born to be a mother, it was amazing. Olivia [her spouse A.P.] went back to work after seven months and I stayed at home with the kids. I fell into motherhood as if I was born for motherhood.

The depiction of motherhood as a fateful destiny, often received further validation through the mystification strategy. Nora (a non-biological mother of a three-year-old in her early 30s), for example, said that since age 14 she would have dreams about pregnancies, labor, and births for years. In her dreams, she would meet her future child and communicate with him. The dreams made her very happy and she would wake up feeling in ecstasy:

Since age 14, I've had dreams of childbirth, of pregnancies. I would dream that I was in my ninth month and I would dream about contractions. It was like that for years upon years... and they were amazing dreams. Oh, I also had some dreams where I actually dreamt that I was communicating with the fetus in my stomach, smelling him/her. No, the gender was not defined. I could really see the eye color, feel the hands, smell the scent and... I really felt like I had met my future child! And when I was in high school, I had a lot of dreams of contractions and childbirth. I would wake up in ecstasy! Elated!

In addition to describing motherhood as fulfilling a destiny, the narrators described their motherhood as an integral part of their essence and identity. Lily spoke about how motherhood was a significant part of her identity even before she became an actual mother. That was reflected in the fact that she always enjoyed spending time with children and playing with them, so much so that her parents' friends thought she'd have a career as a kindergarten teacher. According to her, had she not actually become a mother, she wouldn't have fulfilled an essential part of her identity:

All my life, I saw myself as a mother! I always liked little kids so much, I would always be playing with all the kids. Everyone always told me... my parents' friends would tell me, "She'll be a kindergarten teacher for sure!" For me, it was part of my identity long before I actually became a mother. It was clear to me that... on the contrary – if

I wouldn't become a mother, then I probably wouldn't have – then a part of myself wouldn't have been realized, because it's a part of my identity, as I perceive it to be.

Dori (a biological mother to a 3-year-old girl in her late 30s) described herself as "100% mom" and described motherhood as something that "burns in her bones":

I'm ready and want kids, I... It (clicking her tongue), it burns in my bones! I... I had a difficult pregnancy and a difficult birth, and the moment after I gave birth and one minute before I fainted, because I fainted after giving birth, I said, "Let's go, we're going to do another one." Like, I'm very much a mom, I'm 100% mom!

Similarly, Sarah (an adoptive mother to a 3-year-old girl in her early 40s who immigrated to Israel) saw motherhood as fulfilling her essence as a person, and as a woman. According to her, before the transition to motherhood, she felt unfulfilled and detached from femininity and the world of women, and as she transitions to motherhood, she feels self-fulfillment and closeness to other women around her:

You could say that Naomi [Sarah's daughter, A.P.] helped me enter the world of motherhood. Because suddenly, suddenly there's something to talk about... Like, I got Naomi at a late age. Until then, I felt distanced from... let's just say, the women in the world, because... I felt some kind of unrealized thing that I really wanted to realize as a mother. Now, I've gotten closer to the femininity in the world, to the women in the world, and like, I share this experience of what it's like to be a mother with all the women around me.

In Israeli society, family life plays a central and particularly important role (Fogel-Bizhawi, 1999). The narrators' use of "motherhood" as a benchmark (rather than a criterion of "sexual orientation") to define what a "good woman" is, has facilitated their attempt to reconstruct themselves as normal, valuable women, and to transition from the social sidelines to the mainstream.[37]

> *Some narrators have expressed surprise and even criticism of women — straight or lesbian — who choose not to become mothers. Such criticisms have reaffirmed antiquated divisions between "valued women" (i.e. "mothers") and "less valued women" (i.e. "non-mothers"), and has also formed new divisions between "good lesbian women" (i.e. "lesbian mothers") and "bad lesbian women" (i.e. "non-mother lesbians") (Hequembourg 2012).*

According to Zara (a biological mother of an 8-year-old girl and a non-biological mother to a 6-year-old girl, in her mid-40s), motherhood is the "entrance ticket" of women, including lesbian women, to society. Her transition to motherhood and to family life has given her permission to step out of the social sidelines and enter the "big family called 'society,'" while those who are marginalized and labeled as "outsiders" are women (straight or lesbian) who have chosen not to have children:

> *As soon as... it doesn't matter if you're straight, it doesn't matter... if you had a child — society looks at you differently. You're already a part, part of society. You're not something weird anymore. If a woman says that she hasn't given*

---

37. Efrat, 1999 [Hebrew]; Lieblich, 2009 [Hebrew]; Tzidkiyahu, 2004 [Hebrew]; Ben-Ari and Efrat, 2002; Ben-Ari and Livni, 2006.

birth at all, it will seem awfully strange to people, even more so than her saying she lives with a female partner. People can't accept that people sometimes choose to live alone. But really alone. No children, no one. I even find it difficult to accept. I think about how society accepts me. Obviously, the moment you give birth, you become accepted into the big family called 'society.' And those who choose not to really are the outsiders, the undefined. Society will always look at them differently.

Zara went on to describe her own ambivalent attitude toward women (straight or lesbian) who choose not to be mothers:

Let's just say that until a few years ago, as a lesbian, I couldn't accept the idea that a woman doesn't give birth. It seemed very unusual to me. Like really weird. I think it's really natural, like I'm also like this. It's hard for me to understand why someone would choose to live alone, why they would do that to themselves. Why not have a child? Especially women, who can give birth alone. You don't even need a man. Go to the bank, take some sperm and... Why, why be left alone? What kind of choice is that? Where does it come from, where does this notion of living alone come from? It's very depressing to me. Such a life of deprivation... Today I am able to be friends with someone like that. It used to be so unusual to me that I couldn't even be friends with a woman like that. I used to look at it like, "What is that, it's too weird for me." But today I can be her friend. Like Shirley, our neighbor. She lives with a boyfriend who has children of his own, but she chose not to have any. She's my age and she chose not to give birth. And I love her and accept her like that. But it still always seems like she missed out to me. I'll always look at it like, "What a shame, why not? What do you care? Have at least one child. Like, isn't it a shame? You'll reach age sixty and you won't regret it?" I don't know...

The presence and availability of the mother is another criterion in the patriarchal mother ideal and is even more emphasized in the ideologies of "motherhood essentialism." According to these ideologies, mothers must be at their children's disposal at all times, invest the best of their time, money and energy in raising and caring for the children, and ideally, even be a "full-time mother."[38] The criterion of presence and availability in the children's lives is found to be one of the foremost principles of the maternal ideal of middle-class heterosexual mothers in Israel (Shayovitz-Gurman, 2009).

Although the vast majority of the narrators (36 out of 40 – 90% of the total) were employed at the time of the interview, most reported that they finish work at convenient times (until 5:00 p.m.) so as to allow time for childcare. Demonstrating presence and availability to children is a value that the narrators tended to emphasize and show in their accounts. Talia (a non-biological mother to an 8-year-old boy and 4-year-old boy, and a biological mother to a 2.5-year-old boy, in her early 30s) made it a point to mention that her job allows her to get home by lunchtime and spend plenty of time with the children. Her partner also comes home early. They did not enroll the two older boys in an after-school program, thinking that they should be with them; Only the youngest son goes to an after-school program regularly, at his request:

---

38. DiQuinzio, 1999; Hequembourg, 2012.

All in all, I work a comfortable job in terms of hours for raising children and I could be with Tom [the eldest son, A.P.] a lot and... to this day I am able to be with the children a lot and it's such a pleasure. I really enjoy being with the kids. On an average day... I try to leave for work at 6:30 am, many times it's only a quarter to seven. I start working at 7:30 am and finish at around 1:00 pm. If it's not a busy period. If it is, then I can leave at 2:00p, 3:00p tops. No... It's not something I need to stay too long for. And I get home early. I usually get home at 2:00p. Either I pick the children up from kindergarten or Norma Lee [my partner, A.P.] does, we meet here, eat lunch. Uh... Shawn, the youngest son, really likes to be in the nursery, so we decided not to break up his routine, he stays, he is the only one of the children who has a whole day, a full day. Tom – we never left him, Ron – him neither – and Shawn hmm... he asked to stay from the beginning and we let him, we really let go of the reins with him. We weren't so off-hands with the older boys. We didn't let go at all. Now, every time Ron asks to go to the after-school program, we let him, but we don't sign them up for it in advance. No... only after Ron begged a bunch did we put him and Tom in the program once a week. We think the children should be with us!

Zara criticized straight couples who spend most of the day working outside the home, leaving the care and education of their children in the hands of the kindergarten teacher or grandmother. What can be perceived as a typical work-family conflict, Zara sees in terms of sexual identity – heterosexual parents are parents who do not devote much of their time to their children, and Zara, a lesbian mother, devotes all her free time to raising her children:

There are straight couples who, since they're at work so much, barely see their children. The children are constantly in frameworks. Like my sister's daughter. She serves in a permanent position, and he serves in a permanent position, they both work in the army... Most of the day, it's the grandmother who raises the children. And if the grandmother doesn't, the kids stay in the after-school program sometimes until 5:00p or 6:00p. What kind of life is this? I can't fathom a child growing up like this. Why bring them into this world? For them to be in frameworks all day? And what, what will it give me? Another 500, 700, 900 dollars? That's what will give me the... but a ton of straight people live that way. A ton. Children in frameworks all day long. And grandmothers...

Nellie (a biological mother of a 4-year-old daughter and 2-year-old son in her late 20s) stressed that she and her partner are "all-in mothers," from the beginning to this day. This is reflected, among other things, in the fact that they raise their children in a homeschooling environment. They share the burden of care and education of their children equally:

The fact is, we have both been all-in mothers from a very young age... It was very clear to us from the very first moment. And Raya [her partner, A.P.] also took a month's maternity leave. So we were really able to be together... We homeschool them, and we plan to continue homeschooling them. As far as we're concerned, they should stay at home as long as possible. I believe it will be possible. And we actually split the time half and half with the kids. Half the week I'm with them, half the week Raya's with them. They're not in any frameworks. We're in a place where it's fun for us to be with the children.

Ruddick (1989, 2005) indicated at least three interests that underlie "maternal thinking": Preserving the child's life, nurturing the child's growth, and shaping a valued and socially accepted child. Echoes of each of these interests are later heard in the narrators' remarks.

The narrators reported that they invest in optimal care for their children's basic needs (security and protection, nutrition, sleep, touch, hygiene, and health). Special emphasis was placed on breastfeeding and maintaining a healthy diet, in accordance with middle-class standards and fashionable trends such as the bohemian bourgeoisie.

Arielle (a biological mother of a 1-year-old baby in her early 30s) described herself as a "breastfeeding fanatic" and a "health food fanatic." She has replaced browsing LGBTQ forums with parenting and babies' forums, and is currently a member of a breastfeeding group and a natural mothers group:

> *I've become a bit of a fanatic over the last few years. A breastfeeding and health food fanatic. Like if I used to read pride forums, now I read parenting and baby forums, of which there are several. There's a breastfeeding group that I'm a member of, and there's a group for kids who are around the same age who were all born around the same three month span, and there's a group for natural moms. I'm a member of a lot of groups.*

In addition to protecting the children and taking care of their physical needs, the narrators described themselves as "ideal mothers ," who foster their children's growth in all areas: Emotional, intellectual, physical, and social. This concern is consistent with one of the essential principles of the maternal ideal: "Dedicated physical care and emotional support," as understood by middle-class heterosexual mothers in Israel (Shayo-vitz-Gurman, 2009).

Fostering children's emotional growth is expressed in the narrator's accounts through physical (hugs, kisses) or verbal (saying "I love you") expressions of love to the children, as well as encouraging emotional discourse, which is based on identifying and expressing emotions. Raya (a non-biological mother of a 4-year-old girl and 2-year-old boy in her late 30s) highlighted the central role she places on educating and nurturing her children's emotional intelligence, compared to other parents who invest in nurturing their children's appearance. According to her, emotional education is what helps children be tough and resilient in life. Following this, even though her children are still young, she tells them how she feels, and encourages them to share their feelings with her and to ask her questions:

I believe very, very strongly that the impact of education and the environment is very, very great compared to the genome, the genetics. I believe that there's something obviously genetic that people are born with, but I... being an educator and based on what I see, believe that how you're educated – is what you go out into the world with. People are so busy combing the girl's hair in the morning and giving her the perfect pigtails that they haven't even asked her how she feels. How did you get up this morning. Meaning, the essence, the things that give you resilience in life, is not going to be those pigtails. It's nice when a girl has pigtails, but that's not what's going to help her get through the day. The children get from me a lot of boundaries, a lot of confidence, a lot of talking about their feelings. Even though they're extremely young, I keep talking to them about what they're feeling, what

I'm feeling. Other people's feelings, or something they see. Situations. They are children that ask a lot of questions, they are very curios. I enjoy answering them and also challenging and teaching them. And a lot of the time they want to hear what I have to say and ask me for more. They often ask, "What did she say?" "What is she talking about?" They're interested in what we're talking about or about what I talk about with other people.

Sharon (a biological mother of a 10-year-old boy and 7-year-old girl in her late 40s) noted that the relationship between her and her children is based on intimate conversations on a daily basis. She and her partner make sure to have family dinners during which every family member talks about how their day went. According to her, her children see her as someone to turn to share and consult about unpleasant experiences:

I have an extremely close relationship with my children. On the level of having a lot of daily one-on-one conversations. We also have a conversation every evening at the dinner table. It's the type of conversation where each person talks about how their day went and if they have something unique to share, and we ask questions about their friends and who they played with that day and what they found interesting. So we have that conversation. I think they tell me everything, like it's a very, very personal connection, and very ... It's an all-day thing, we talk all day. I think they also feel comfortable coming to talk to me and tell me about bad things. Nate, for example, comes home from school one day and says to me, "Mom, I want to talk to you about something, I want to talk to you alone." Okay, so I go to his room with him, and he tells me that he was playing with two girls from his class that day during recess and one of the girls told the other that she feels bad and wanted to kill herself. And that's what he told me. So I started asking a few questions to gauge whether those were her exact words or if it was what he understood from what she said, to know if that's exactly what she said and if he quoted correctly... It led to a phone call to the teacher to see where it was coming from and to bring it to the attention of the guidance counselor...

The cognitive-intellectual domain is another area the narrators have invested in in nurturing their children's growth. Nora described how she and her partner foster their 3-year-old son intellectually, and the fruits of their investment expressed in the form of a "gifted child." According to her, she and her partner expose their son to a large and rich vocabulary, teach him how to count, read books to him, and as a result, he knows how to count to ten, is familiar with colors and synonyms, can distinguish right from left, and has musical knowledge. As a testament to their educational success, Nora cites the "voice" of her parents (the non-biological grandparents), who never cease to admire his knowledge, wisdom, and sensitivity and wonder "what he'll do in first grade":

He's very musical, very... and smart! Since he was a year and 10 months old, we've had magnets of all the numbers and all the ... so he knows how to say all the words, all the numbers, all the colors, all of it. He's just a year and 10 months... and he knows how to count to ten all on his own, he knows right from left, he like knows how to use plurals and after he goes a little wild, he wants to sit down and he says, "I'll rest a little while." And he asks me, "Are you resting, will you rest, too?" Like, "If you're tired, go rest in your bed," or "Are you thirsty? I'll bring you some water." I'm very into ... talking to him, you know, like an adult using a high register and he answers accordingly... The child knows, I taught him synonyms: For instance, a vehicle can be a vehicle or a car. He knows that there are a few words for everything. Like (she laughs), like there isn't... he's something! Gifted! (knocks on wood). My parents really enjoy him, they're ecstatic about him, and they say, "That's it, he's the best grandson... There's, he's... there's no one like him, just amazing!" My mom says to me, "Tell me, what, what's he going to do in 1st grade?" They tell me he's so smart and sensitive and... his emotional intellect, his emotional intelligence is so developed and he, he just gets things...

Ruddick (1989, 2005) described the concept of raising a valued and socially acceptable child as one of the prominent interests that underlies the "maternal thinking" of all mothers. The narrators in this book attributed unique importance to ensuring that children don't feel insecure, hurt, or rejected by their peers, due to their family differences. As a result, they invested a great deal of time, resources, and effort (often at the expense of their own time, privacy, and freedom) in fostering their children's social lives, often hosting children's friends in their homes, and encouraging their children to participate in parties, activities, and social events. At the same time, they pointed out the acceptance and sympathy their children receive, both from adults (educators, parents of children) and from their peers. These claims helped them defend themselves against cultural accusations that lesbian mothers "condemn" their children to a life of social "disgrace," isolation, and rejection, impairing their emotional and social development,[39] and helped them reposition

---

39. Hequemberg, 2012; Kranz and Daniluk, 2002.

themselves as "worthy mothers" raising healthy, accepted, and socially valued children.

Perry (a biological mother of a 4-year-old girl in her late 30s) described the effort she and her partner invest in fostering their daughter's social life so that she "doesn't feel like she's abnormal" and "has a normal childhood." This effort is expressed in managing and maintaining an active agenda for her daughter, which includes scheduling frequent social get-togethers, participating in afternoon classes, and attending plays, even at the cost of missing out on quiet time, privacy, and maintaining a good connection with her parents, all of which doesn't particularly interest her so much:

We are very invested in the social aspect... like... that she'll always be surrounded by people and family and friends and classes and plays... we've been taking her, I think, ever since she was a year old or so, she's in plays all the time, really like... she's a very, very active girl. It's really important to me that my daughter doesn't feel like she's different! (raises her voice). Even if it manifests itself like this, where we invest more and more in her. Like, for me personally, I'm telling you, I love my quiet, I love when, you know, you come home and you have peace and quiet to yourself. But I know that she needs the social life, she needs the activity. So, I really try all the time to schedule time for her with the kids, with parents. I have no problem making the connections, but sometimes I find myself communicating with parents I don't even feel like talking to, I don't feel like talking, they don't interest me, but so that my girl can play with friends... Like, I find myself somehow adjusting to the other parents, so that, you know, the child doesn't feel like she's abnormal, so that she has a normal childhood...

Olivia (a biological mother of a 10-year-old boy and an eight-year-old girl in her late 40s) said that she and her partner have dinners and host the children's friends at their home. The kids also like to stay with their friends. At the same time, she emphasized that the children are very popular, they don't feel like they are different (e.g. they don't check "if they have horns") and are not treated differently or abused by their peers (e.g. they're not called "gay"), at least not at this stage:

> *We host, we really like to have dinners and entertain. Sometimes there are friends of the children, sometimes they go over to friends, some TV, some computer time. All in all, they don't feel like they're different to the point where they're checking if they have horns growing on top of their heads. They are very accepted, they have friends, and we host here a lot. They don't feel, you know, they're not treated differently either. They aren't called "gay" or, you know, like kids can be... maybe at an older age, when they get older, but now there isn't...*

Furthermore, many narrators emphasize the central role they give their children, even if it harms other aspects of their lives, such as personal growth, relationships, careers, socio-political activism, etc. These arguments are consistent with patriarchal ideologies of "good motherhood" which require a mother to demonstrate exclusive and selfless devotion to her children, and to always put their needs before her own.[40]

Confirmation of the narrators' stances regarding placing the children's needs at the center of their lives can be found in longitudinal studies that followed children raised in lesbian families throughout their childhood, adolescence, and as they become

---

40. Shayovitz-Gurman, 2009 [Hebrew]; O'Reilly, 2004.

young adults. Throughout their development, the children reported greater availability, involvement, and emotional investment on behalf of their mothers compared with children in heterosexual family units.[41]

Rachel (a non-biological mother of a 1-year-old baby in her early 40s) noted that since the birth of her child, motherhood became a dominant aspect of her identity and impacts her behavior more than anything: Lesbian sexuality, desires, personal expression, and so on. According to her, the transition to motherhood transformed her from a selfish and self-centered woman to one who looks at the world through the perspective of her son's eyes and devotes herself to fulfilling his needs. Rachel's words easily correspond with an "anti-lesbian mythology," according to which lesbian women are unfit to be mothers since they are selfish, childish, and underdeveloped.[42] The "personality transformation" process proclaimed by Rachel, helps her reestablish herself as a competent, worthy, and devoted mother:

I am first a mother and then a lesbian. Motherhood has taken on a new dimension, it comes first, before everything, really before anything at all, before myself. I don't know how other women experience it, but I – as a lesbian woman – uh... I experienced something in myself that was very egotistical. "Just me and me alone." Uh... and just my desires and them alone. And suddenly, when a child arrived, all of my "self," all my personal expression, the way I presented myself as "me," shifted a little more to the side. That is to say, I, first and foremost, see myself through Johnny, through my child. And when a mother

---

41. Golombok, et al., 1997; Golombok and Badger, 2010; MacCallum and Golombok, 2004.

42. Hequemberg, 2012; Kranz and Daniluk, 2002

sees herself first through her child, she is first a mother, and then she has a partner, and then she's a lesbian, and then we can talk about sexuality, and then we can talk about interpersonal dynamics. But, I am first and foremost a mom!

Dori, who works as a kindergarten teacher at a daycare, spoke of herself in terms of being "100% mom" in the sense that she devotes herself entirely to caring for her own child and for the children at the daycare in the best possible way, even at the cost of damaging her partnership or neglecting her health and appearance:

I'm very much a mom, I'm 100% mom! I barely... There's a bit of a problem with that because I'm less of a woman of... but I'm 100% mom! Most of the time, I don't really care how I look. The main thing is that you know that everything will be okay, that there will be food. I have snot on me, I have stuff all over me... I take care of the children all day, I'm a mother all day long! I'm busy being a mom the whole day, I play the game of 'mom' all day! I don't go to work outside, I don't dress nicely. I don't have shoes... I have Crocs sneakers (giggles) and hiking sandals. I play "mama" all day, literally all day! It's, I love it, I like enjoy it... again, this comes with some difficulties: I'm less of a woman who... and I have to learn how to do this! I gained weight while I was pregnant and didn't lose it since the birth and it didn't even phase me, until I said to myself, "Get back to yourself, start working on yourself." So I went to the gym, I made an effort! But I'm all mom, totally into it!

Norma Lee (a biological mother of an 8-year-old boy and 2.5-year-old boy, and non-biological mother to a 4-year-old boy in her mid-30s) highlighted that she is a child-oriented mother who puts her children's needs before her own, and chose a job that lets her do that with flexible hours, even though it came at the cost of low pay and lack of professional growth. According to her, even when choosing her next job, which should be more professionally fulfilling, she has her eyes set on being available in the children's lives and involved in raising them:

> *I am a mother who is very child-oriented, I can tell you that I put my children's needs before my own. Until now, part of the choices we had to make when it came to work was to compromise and make a little less money so that we can be there more during our children's early years, which is why we are both at home with the kids at lunchtime. We're precisely at the stage where I'm starting to think about a career that I'll find to be more for myself. To tell you that it's... it will never come at the expense of the children. As long as it's up to me, and we're not in a financial situation where I have to work late at night, I'll still want to come home at a normal time, be with the children, and raise them. What did I bring them into this world for if not to see them?! So I'll say it again, I do think that at this point, at their age, they're a little more important than I am...*

Similarly, Arielle described how her child takes first place in her life, and how her professional aspirations were lowered on the priority list when she transitioned to motherhood:

> *I've been working at my job for four and a half years, and to me, four years is a time to take a good look at your life. You look at what happened, you think about what's next. And I'm not really doing this because I have a child and it's not right for me to start something new now and*

work more hours at a place that might be... I don't know how the place is, like... towards mothers. So I was happy, I have a lot of professional fantasies, and I would like to fulfill them sometimes, but not yet... because right now what's important to me is being with the girl and with the children I will have after her...

The absence of maternal ambivalence is another dominant principle of the maternal ideal for middle-class heterosexual mothers in Israel (Shayovitz-Gurman, 2009). The narrators in the book acted in accordance with this directive, which severely limits women's ability to express negative emotions towards their children (O'Reilly, 2004). In contrast to positive emotions or feelings of guilt that were significantly represented in the majority of the narratives, negative emotions were expressed in marginal narratives or were excluded from the discourse altogether, so as not to damage the primary message of contentment, satisfaction, and complete fulfillment, as embodied in the patriarchal maternal ideal.

Signs of negative emotions towards children and difficulty expressing them are echoed in Dori's words. Dori described how difficult it is for her to express anger or frustration at her daughter's unwanted or inappropriate behavior, Natalie. She said she almost never lost control or acted aggressively toward her daughter. On the few occasions that she behaved more aggressively and firmly (as a result of fatigue and impatience), she experienced feelings of guilt and discomfort. The very act of "talking" about a topic that is too "illegitimate" or "dangerous" to be discussed – in this case, ambivalent feelings toward the daughter – overwhelmed Dori with guilt and anxiety during the interview, so much so that she silenced herself and added the sentence "it's best that parents don't hear this," referring to an imagined audience of parents listening in on her words:

I remember one time when Natalie was younger and she was at my daycare, she bit another child and it made me very angry. That was the only time I was very angry with her, I didn't lose control, but I was very angry with her. I don't like to be angry... I remember there were nights when she drove me crazy and she couldn't stop crying... She wanted something... And I couldn't stand it anymore and I was so tired, I was so tired then. The loss of control was... I was assertive, I told her, "Natalie, go to sleep, I'm tired! Go to sleep, already!" And then I went to Amy, my partner, "but I told her to go to sleep already." And Amy was actually pleased, "Good, for once she'll see that you're assertive!" But I felt uncomfortable, like... I didn't lose control, but I was assertive and very firm, because I was so tired already, so tired – I wanted to sleep and that girl wouldn't stop babbling at me. So there's that. A little annoying and all that, I know. It's honestly best for parents not to hear this.

Daria (a biological mother of a 6-year-old boy in her late 30s) used the metaphor of "super glue" to describe her relationship with her son. The metaphor is a figurative means of discussing experiences that cannot otherwise be discussed (Gilligan and Brown, 1992). On the one hand, the metaphor of "glue" and describing him as a "family child" who needs her presence all the time can indicate a strong relationship of love and closeness, but on the other, can also express dependence and inseparability, to the point that sometimes "you feel like shoving him off":

The relationship between me and Ian – super glue doesn't even stand a chance against it. He also bonded with Jasmine [A.P.] really strongly. He wants us all together at all times. He... He's a kid like that, a family child, he doesn't like... I go to the pool with him, I need to be with him. He goes to take a shower, sleep, all of it is together. He is glue. Sometimes you feel like, you know, shoving, but he doesn't let go so quickly. He'll probably grow up. Either he will or he won't. But he's a very sensitive kid. He's amazing. A cute boy. And, you know, I think also... I don't know. We were glued together from the beginning. We're a pretty glue-y family. What can we do?

Constructing value and respectability – differentiation and branding, emphasizing the advantages of lesbian relationships and parenting

While employing the strategy of demonstrating obedience to the patriarchal maternal ideal and highlighting the similarities between them and heterosexual mothers, the narrators employed a contrasting and complementary strategy of negotiating with the patriarchal maternal ideal, differentiating themselves from heterosexual mothers, and highlighting the unique strengths of lesbian relationships and motherhood.

These strengths included a marital relationship based on an authentic choice to be together and respectful communication, shared decision-making and an equal division of roles, shared concern for the children's upbringing and their mental well-being, an absence of violence or neglect, unconditional love and acceptance, fostering resilience, pride and uniqueness among the children, exposing them to tasks independent of gender roles, encouraging the children to experience diverse gender practices, and educating them on the values of asking questions, and being open and tolerant. While the first strategy helped them construct themselves as normal, normative women and mothers ("We are as good as heterosexual mothers"), the second strategy helped them position and brand themselves as respectable women and mothers with added value ("We are better than heterosexual mothers").

Many of the narrators described their relationship as an exemplary model, reflecting free will and authentic choice, and based on friendship, mutual understanding, trust, and respectful communication. Marital relationships in lesbian families have often been portrayed as the antithesis of the fakeness, hypocrisy, oppression, and alienation to which the narrators were exposed to as young girls and adolescents growing up in heterosexual families.

Toby (a non-biological mother of a 4-year-old girl and a biological mother of a 2-year-old girl in her mid-40s) emphasized friendship, trust, openness, sharing, identification, and emotional support in her relationship with her partner:

> *My partner is my friend, she's my best friend. She knows... I tell her everything that happens to me, with me, and in general, all my secrets, she is my counselor. We share so much information, moments, and experiences together, both things we go through together and things we go through alone, with incredible openness. She tells me about her past and I tell her about mine, you know. We cry together, we're happy together, we love together, we're sad together. Everything. She's my friend, my best friend, it's the most fun thing in the world to spend with her. She also has incredible intuition, which I've learned to, you know, trust to a degree. She... I trust her like I don't trust anyone else in my life.*

Rona used the accepted essentialist distinctions of "women are from Venus" and "men are from Mars" to point out the "natural" advantages of same-sex female vs. heterosexual relationships:

My choice to live with a woman, besides the fact that she is right for me, is, in my opinion, the right choice, period. I have yet to encounter a heterosexual woman who , with genuine honesty not to manipulate, with genuine honesty, told me, "Sometimes, I envy you a little." We are all from Venus, and they are all from Mars. Naturally, when we are all from one planet, we speak the same language, we understand each other better, our life is simpler together than living with a man. Like The Drama of the Gifted Child, this, to me, is The Drama of the Heterosexual Woman...

Dori described her and her partner's relationship as the antithesis of her parents' relationship, which was full of lies and secrets:

I think our children will live better than I did with my mom and dad. I think that what I'm building here with Amy, what we're building together, is a warm and loving nest, with dialogue, with understanding, with insights. We can disagree, and within that also live, compromise, see each other, feel each other, hear each other, listen. I think there's something different between a man and a woman, the relationship is different. The lies and secrets my mother hid from my father or my father from my mother, created something else. The communication was different, I can say that, I can see it. And here I feel like we're creating something different. Anything can be, I'm not saying it's forever, I don't know, anything can happen. But whatever it is, it's with understanding and with respect and a desire to be good and a desire to empower each other.

Perry spoke about how she exposes her daughter to a serene, steady, and harmonious relationship, in contrast to the quarrels and arguments she was exposed to in her childhood home, thereby promoting her daughter's mental health, compared to the family conditions she grew up in. For Perry, the formula is clear – it's better for a child to grow up in a harmonious household with two mothers and no father, than in a conflict-ridden home with a father and mother:

> *Personally, I know I had a father and a mother and I had a lot of fun with my father and I was very attached to him, but still the relationship between my parents was not one of harmony. There was shouting and fighting and arguments, and sometimes I would find myself telling my parents, "get a divorce!" because how much can you fight?! So I know it's... even if children have their mom and dad and they live together, it still doesn't mean they'll grow up in a normal home or be normal. So maybe my child will grow up without a father instead of in a house with a mom and a dad, but there won't be any fights or arguments and... and she won't lack of anything! Also, a woman can often give more and invest more than a man...*

Same-sex female partnerships were portrayed by the narrators as having unique advantages compared to heterosexual couples, in terms of decision-making, cooperation in raising the children, and division of roles within the family. According to the narrators, the foundation of the "marital contract" in same-sex families is the partnership they have with their partners in all matters related to household tasks and childcare. This partnership included three aspects: The **functional aspect** – active and equal participation as much as possible in home maintenance and childcare; the **emotional aspect** – emotional commitment and responsibility of both mothers; and the **mental-managerial aspect** – joint thinking and decision-making.

Validation of these characteristics of same-sex partnerships can be found in various studies in Israel and around the world, that examined issues including division of roles, style of decision-making, and childcare in lesbian families. Studies in the Western world show that mothers in same-sex families are characterized by shared decision-making and an equal and flexible division of roles in all matters related to household tasks and childcare.[43]

In Israel, it was also found that the division of roles in lesbian families was more equal compared to that of heterosexual couples. Also, the non-biological mother in lesbian relationships tended to take a more active role in childcare, compared to the biological father in heterosexual relationships (Or, 2000).

The way the narrators put it, the experience of partnership among spouses/mothers is expressed, first and foremost, in the active and equal participation of both spouses/mothers in maintaining the home and in caring for the children (which is generally combined with work ending in the afternoon). This active and egalitarian cooperation was understood in sharp contrast to the asymmetrical gendered division of roles in heterosexual marriages, whereby the father is the primary breadwinner who spends most of the day away from home, and the mother bears most of the burden at home of maintenance and childcare (whether she works or not).

Lily emphasized her and her partner's equal investment in a variety of aspects related to children rearing: Therapeutic, educational, and experiential. She argues that the equal division between her and her partner allows her to bear the burden of childcare more easily than a straight woman who is solely responsible for childcare, as though she were a "single mother":

---

43. Bos, et al., 2005; Patterson, 1995

I think, in general, for the normal, average straight mom – what I see with my friends – the burden is much greater! because usually, the man, her partner, does a lot less and she just does more... I mean, I feel like I'm doing everything with my children, but the division is still, the division is more equal! I mean, there are times when I will do the work and times when Ella will do the work. We basically do the same thing: Hang out with the kids in the afternoon, take care of them... like, in the fun way and in the study way and in the therapeutic way – I do the same thing, but I feel like in smaller doses. In other words, it's not like the whole burden falls on me. It's more equal. I just know a lot of couples where the man comes home very late from work. We have good friends where the husband owns a sushi restaurant, so he's just never there! he's only home on weekends because he's at his restaurant from 12:00 noon until 2:00 in the morning. So she's basically a single parent! she does everything alone!

Heidi illustrated the gap between the level of commitment, cooperation, and participation among heterosexual couples and her relationship. According to her, while the heterosexual woman is busy with the "operational management" of her partner all the time ("clear the table, wash the dishes, take out the garbage"), the cooperation between her and her partner is "natural" and automatic ("you don't have to say a word") – harmonious and effective. The reconceptualization of lesbian couples as "normal" and "natural" takes on a special meaning of a "reversal of values" in a sociocultural context in which lesbian relationships are usually "marked" as "pathological" and "unnatural":

For me, being a woman raising children with a partner is the most normal, ordinary, and natural thing. Any other way wouldn't seem natural to me. You don't have to tell anyone what to do, you don't have to press "start" for a person to start functioning and then "stop" when you want them to stop, because he sees the garbage but won't throw it away. And we're very much in a straight community, so I see exactly what goes on. Most of our friends are straight actually. So you see how it is. You have to tell him to take out the garbage, you have to tell him to wash the dishes, you have to tell him to clear the table, because he comes home from work and sits in front of the TV and watches the sports channel. And here you don't have to talk, you really don't have to say a word, because things get done.

Arielle emphasized the glaring loneliness of heterosexual mothers compared to the shared approach and decision-making of lesbian ones:

Most of the time, straight women do things alone. That is, they are the ones who have to make the decisions. There is someone who helps, but they are the foundation... It seems extremely difficult to raise children when you are the only person responsible for everything. And I think that when you're in such a situation, you can often find yourself making decisions you're not necessarily at peace with, just because you don't have anyone to think it through enough with. You have to make the decision right now, because if you don't, then no one will, and many times this results in decisions that aren't necessarily right.

According to Raya, there is less stress in a lesbian relationship, while the division of roles in straight families is clear and pre-structured according to gender, and there is no dialogue and discussion around desires, needs, and preferences:

> *It seems to me that in lesbian relationships, there is less stress and more room to bring what everyone believes in to the table, what everyone wants to do. It seems to me that in straight families it's just... um... There's this kind of division of roles, one that appears to be self-evident, which is very stressful, because, like, no one talks about: What is convenient for each of the parties; what is good for each spouse? Um... And the social roles are also very, very clear. The man is the breadwinner, the woman is supposed to be responsible for the children. And that's how it is.*

Adriana (a non-biological mother of a 9-year-old boy, a 5-year-old girl, and a 1-year-old boy in her early 50s) described the drastic shifts in her and her partner's parental roles over the years, amid changes in the division of time of work-home balance. According to her, parental identity is a "fluid" one that can be "loaded" with many meanings and complex possibilities that go far beyond gender and biology:

> *I study psychology, work a lot in therapy, and I'm also a therapist myself, so... This is an area that interests me very much, and the question "Wait, am I a mother or a father?" always comes up with my therapist, as a practical question that goes beyond my sexual identity or beyond... I mean, "What is my role in the family?" and it seems to me that this is actually something fluid. I mean, take us for example, there were certain times when we went from being "two moms" to what might be "mom and dad," and then I was more of a "dad" in my role, and now Hellen, my spouse, is more of a "dad" in her role, because I'm more at*

home with the kids. It's something completely fluid. But
we remain two parents. That's what matters.

At the same time, many narrators emphasized their and their partner's well-developed emotional intelligence and shared concern for their children's health and well-being. They used essentialist gender stereotypes that identify "femininity" with a "developed therapeutic ability" and "maternal concern" to construct themselves as "good mothers."

The developed therapeutic ability of both spouses/mothers and their shared commitment to the emotional health of their children, were expressed in the active involvement of both mothers in the children's lives, through acknowledging the children's emotions and responding to their distress, and through the absence of neglect, harm and abuse. These characteristics and practices have often been constructed against the lack of emotional intelligence and neglect, abandonment, abuse, or violence among heterosexual families with men/fathers.

Evidence of the narrators' claims can be found in studies that examined the relationship between mothers and children in lesbian family units. According to the results of these studies, children and adolescents, growing up in lesbian families in the United States and Europe, reported a higher degree of availability, involvement, and emotional investment on behalf of the mothers (Golombok and Badger, 2010), and a lack of exposure to physical violence and sexual abuse (Gartrell et al., 2011), compared with children and adolescents growing up in heterosexual family units.

Nora noted that she feels fortunate to be a woman raising a child in a same-sex relationship. In addition to her experience of being understood and accepted by her partner and having an equal partnership in carrying the burden, she emphasizes that their child has a significant advantage over other kids, because

he receives warmth, love, and devotion from two parental figures and doesn't grow up in a family constellation where there's
usually a caring mother and an "indifferent father":

> *I think I'm lucky. I see a lot of straight women who are very*
> *busy resenting the fact that the man isn't around, and*
> *being a mom – it falls on them, how fun it would be if they*
> *could be with a woman. And I feel like I'm very understood*
> *and accepted. And that the child, you know, the warmth*
> *and the love he receives from another person, having*
> *another woman who cares deeply for him and cares oh so*
> *much, and not some indifferent father...*

Nora went on to highlight that in the framework of a family
with two female parents, it is rare to find occurrences of neglect,
abandonment, addiction, or abuse, while in heterosexual families these phenomena are not uncommon. According to her, in
her work as a therapist, she has witnessed many cases in which
the parents divorced and the father abandoned the child in order to turn over a "new leaf." She emphasizes that "a woman
is always a mother," and thus will never abandon or voluntarily give up her children unless she is dealing with severe mental
health issues, is in a psychiatric hospital, addicted to drugs, or
incarcerated in prison. Her words imply that there is utter overlap between feminine and maternal identity, and that as such,
the commitment of each woman to her maternal role is abso-
lute (except in abnormal, tragic cases), while for men, that same
overlap or commitment doesn't necessarily exist:

> *It's very rare, I don't even know if it exists, a female couple*
> *with a child – where the child experiences abuse at home*
> *or addiction from one of the partners, abandonment*
> *and all that. Like, it almost never happens! a woman –*

abandoning her child?! let's say they divorce and she abandons the child – yeah right! like, it's motherhood! these days, do you know how often I treat children whose father divorced the wife and simply abandoned the child?! to just get up and go! he doesn't care about the child at all – from a financial standpoint, from the standpoint of just being there, talking to him. Like, a woman would never give up on her child like that – it could be that she is in a very, very bad mental state and voila, hospitalized somewhere. I don't know... or because she's in prison, because she's addicted to drugs. I think these are the only options for a woman – only if she has very serious mental issues. Besides, a woman would never... you know, just cut him out and turn over a new leaf somewhere. It's a child! a woman is a mother! always and forever!

In addition, the narrators tended to emphasize characteristics such as non-judgmental treatment, unconditional love, and acceptance of their children as major advantages of their parenting. The narrators' words implied that the lack of judgment and the acceptance they provide their children with, is largely due to their ability to accept their own sexual differences. At the same time, they were able to say how critical parental acceptance and unconditional love are to a child's sense of security and mental health, given their personal experience of having to cope with homophobia and rejection in the family and in the social environment.

For Sherry (a non-biological mother of a 10-year-old boy and 7-year-old girl in her late 40s), it is very important that the children perceive the family and home as stable and strong "pillars" in their lives, an experience she did not have herself. She declared that she and her partner would stand by their children in

any situation and under any conditions and would never abandon them, even if they became criminals, and on the other end
of things, even if they were homosexual:

> *It's very important for me to let the children know that they
> have, for example, and this is something I wasn't raised
> with, that their home is their anchor, that their home is
> their place of support, no matter what, they always know
> that Sharon [her spouse, A.P.] and I will be there for them
> no matter what. Oh, and that's something that's very, very
> important to me, it's something I didn't grow up with,
> that I didn't have. Um... and that's something I try very,
> very hard to instill in them, that they know that no matter
> what, as long as we're here, that they can rest assured that
> we'll be there for them in any situation. I know that no
> matter what my child does, I will always stand by him,
> not in terms of justifying what he has done, but I will
> stand by him in such a way that I will give him all the
> help I can. God forbid, if my child would be a criminal, I
> wouldn't throw him out or say, "You're not my child," or if
> tomorrow my child decides to be gay, then I wouldn't say...*

Similarly, Arielle pointed out that she aspires to be a mother
who sees her daughter as a whole, independent, and separate
person, and respects her worldview and choices, unlike her own
mother, who opposed her marrying a woman ("To her, it was
the worst thing I could've done, that or marrying an Arab") and
wanted to impose her values and choices on her. According to
her, if her daughter prefers to be an ultra-Orthodox woman in
a world where she will be oppressed as a woman, it could pose
a serious challenge for her, yet she believes that she will overcome the difficulty and not distance herself. In fact, even if her
daughter becomes a serial killer, she wouldn't cut ties with her.

To a large extent, Arielle's words echo the hierarchy of marginal identities in Israeli society, where minorities are discriminated against, based on nationalism, racism, religion, and gender, and compete with each other for recognition, equality, and worth:

> *I would be very happy if my daughter would come to me with anything... From a place where, when I was 16, 17, or 22, that's not how I felt... My mother wasn't like that. As far as she's concerned, I have to do what my mother thinks. And I always do the opposite, always do the exact thing she wouldn't do. So I don't want to be like that. I want to be... I mean, I keep thinking like what's the worst thing my child can do... because as far as my mother is concerned, having a same-sex partner is the worst thing I could have done, the worst. It's that or I don't know what, marrying an Arab... Like actually. Those are the worst things. And I tried to think about what these things would be for me that my child would bring home and I wouldn't be able to handle it. So my first answer was that there are no such things. But my second answer is not. My second answer is like, let's say my child would want to be ultra-Orthodox, it's something I'd have a very hard time with. If my child chooses a world where having big goals isn't as respected, and where there is no equality between individuals... Like if my child wanted to be in a place where she was inferior, it would be very difficult for me. Even then, I think my mother's approach to all these things was very wrong. I think, I know for a fact that when you tell someone they're wrong over and over and over again, they don't start to be right, they just walk away from you. So I hope that even if my child does something that is most unlike me, I will know how to give it the respect it deserves and understand that this is her choice and that now I have to see how I...*

my child could be a serial killer and I still wouldn't cut ties
with her in any way. To make a long story short, I would
like to be a mother, and I think I am like this now, but
like a mother who respects her daughter's experiences and
space and knows that she is not me, that we are not the
same person. We don't have to agree on everything, we
don't have to do the same things.

Other narrators emphasized that they foster a sense of pride and uniqueness among their children. They told their children that they were "the most special children in the world" or that they were their "gifts," and encouraged them to regard otherness and uniqueness as sources of strength, power, and pride. According to them, under such conditions of emotional empowerment, not only do their children not suffer from shame and social rejection, they also become, in certain cases, objects of admiration and envy by friends and acquaintances.

Olivia pointed out that she and her partner raised their children, from the moment they were born, knowing they have no father but have two mothers and are therefore "the most special children in the world." This knowledge accompanies the children as a slogan throughout their growing process, and instills in them strength and pride. At the same time, they treat their children like "gifts" that they received after many years of wishing, efforts, and anticipation to have them in their lives:

The children have known from age zero, we always raised
them to know "how special you are." "You are the most
special children in the world." "You don't have a father
and you have two mothers." It's kind of like a slogan: "You
are the most special children in the world." So they, they've
really grown into it. When we speak to the children about
the differences between us and other families, we tell them

85

that we are a special family, that mom and I have been together for many years and that we wanted children and went to a place, they know what a sperm bank is, and we chose sperm. They are our gift, they are our gift, that we received as a gift.

In some cases, the children's sense of pride and power resonates, and is reflected and reciprocated in their social environments, where their friends envy them, as expressed by Olga (a biological mother of a 5-year-old girl and 3-year-old girl in her late 30s):

There are no same-sex families at the kindergarten we go to, not even any single-parent families, no divorcees, no nothing... it's a bit strange. Even though the kindergarten teacher mentions other families on Family Day, it's still not... they still don't laugh at them or anything... they don't feel... they do feel that they are different, but more so in the opposite direction. There's a girl in the kindergarten, for example, who is very jealous of our girls who have two mothers...

Olga went on to argue that as her daughters get older, they will have to recognize that there are people who find it difficult to accept their family differences and will have to deal with less sympathetic reactions, but it can also be an opportunity to develop resilience and personal growth and doesn't have to necessarily be a destructive experience:

The girls, you know, are totally in their princess phase and then the prince comes along, and there are no alternatives. So Ava, the eldest, asked me, "But who's your husband?" she didn't ask why we didn't get married. But when it

*comes to it, we'll have to tell them the bitter truth, she'll
understand that there's something sour about this whole
picture. That in society, there are people who don't accept
those who are different from them. It's a reality they need
to know about. I think it will help them mature, too, you
know? I see the picture from both sides. But it's a matter
of coping with something, that will likely shape and
strengthen them.*

There were narrators who mentioned that they present a division of roles to their children that doesn't differentiate "feminine" from "masculine" roles, that is based on skills, personal
preferences, needs, and life circumstances. According to Gaia
(an adoptive mother of a 4.5-year-old girl in her early 30s from
abroad), her daughter Nadia is exposed to a division of roles in
which she and her partner fulfill all the roles in the house. These
roles include both "feminine" roles such as folding laundry and
cooking, and "masculine" roles such as moving cabinets and
machines, and doing repair work and renovation:

*I guess I'm not a stereotypical mom when it comes to the
mom/dad split. I don't fold laundry, cook: I do everything,
because we both do everything at home! there's no man
here. There is us and we do everything! and it's very
important for me to stress this to Nadia! to point it out to
her every time, even though she sees it: We move things
around, do renovations, hammer, do things that for a
woman living with a man is not very likely to have to
do, that she won't likely encounter such situations. The
washing machine breaks down and she waits for him to
come and fix it! like, it's very clear! Oh, and we don't have
that! I'm happy to let Nadia see that it's possible... at the
moment she's not yet aware about the whole women/men*

divide but that anything is possible! we do everything. There's no one mother does this and the other does that. We both do the same things. And there's like no stereotypical gender issues we have to play by.

Gaia goes on to point out that she and her partner recently made changes in the garage that involved hard and strenuous physical effort, without the help of a man. When they finished the work, it was important for them to call their daughter over to show her the fruits of their joint efforts. What motivated them to call her over was the desire to show her that women can do anything, and that she, too, is fit and worthy of doing anything:

We have a garage that we just made some changes to – we moved a closet, did a lot of physical things that are really hard to do. And we did it step by step, very slowly. If there was a man here, he would have done it in a minute and a half! and we started deliberating, "should we call someone or not call someone," and then we said, "Well, let's see what can be done," and we worked it out in the end. And it was important for me to call Nadia to show her, "Look, Mom and Mommy moved the machine. It was very heavy but we managed to do it in the end! we tried and we succeeded!" something like that. It's very important to me... to give that to her. It has to do with the fact that there is no man here and there is no division of roles of "his" and "hers." I hope that she will take this on, that she will succeed in... that we will succeed in instilling in her this vibe of "you can be whatever you want, whoever you want, however you want to be – anything is possible, everything goes! like, it's all in your hands!"

Similarly, Jordan (a non-biological mother of a 6-month-old boy in her early 30s) mentioned that her and her partner's son was less exposed to gender stereotypes and a gendered division of roles in the family. Since they are both strong, opinionated, and assertive women who divvy up the roles according to skills and preferences, their son will grow up with a more respectful view of women, and their daughter – if they'll have one in the future – will also feel more empowered and less constrained by gender stereotypes, compared to boys and girls raised in typical heterosexual families:

> *My motherhood is different from that of a straight woman. First of all, by the fact that I will be open to any choice he decides to make in life. I believe I'll raise a girl with less female stereotypes of "what you can do" and "what you can't do." I believe that will teach the boy as well, that he'll view women a little differently from how women are perceived, because he lives with two women who don't really play the gender role of "I'm a woman, so I can't do that," "I'm a woman so I won't be assertive, I won't achieve what I want, I won't manage on my own"... I think that beyond the fact that there are no gender roles that are predetermined because we're a man or a woman at home, obviously each of us just does what we're good at, and not what society tells us we have to do.*

While demonstrating equal relationships and non-gendered role divisions among mothers, many of the narrators indicated that they let their children to experience a relatively wide range of gendered roles, activities, and behaviors, including those stereotypically identified with the opposite sex. At the same time, this experience is primarily limited to the private and domestic sphere, and estranged from any socio-political ideology. It was explained in terms of an educational-psychological principle that serves the children's developmental needs and promotes their personal growth.

Emma (a biological mother of a 3-year-old boy in her 30s) said that she plays a range of male and female roles at home, and makes sure to involve her son Andrew in a variety of activities and roles, whether it's cooking a meal or repairing a drawer. At the same time, she lets him experiment with a wide range of toys and accessories (e.g., dolls, necklaces, guns, cars, hammers), costumes and role-playing games (wearing a dress at home as part of a game with his nieces). In her opinion, exposing children to a large variety of games, activities and role-playing games is appropriate for every family, because it allows the children to get to know themselves and make authentic choices at school and work, choices that will eventually turn them into happy, fulfilled, and confident adults. In contrast, conditioning children into rigid gender roles harms their ability to get to know themselves and harms their opportunities for growth:

> From what I see and how I live, there are no roles, no gender division, that is, no things that only boys do and things that only girls do. I am a person who thinks that anyone can do anything, and in my home, I can do everything. I mean, I can cook, iron and sew, and I can fix furniture, fix the wall, and do electrical work, and I actually do everything. And Andrew helps out, he does everything with me. He can stand with me in the kitchen and cook and then go to a toolbox and take out a nail and hammer to fix a drawer that's fallen apart. And if he wants to play with necklaces and dolls, he can, and I won't tell him, "No, don't play with that because it's a girls' game." And if he wants to play with guns and cars, then he'll play with guns and cars, and I won't encourage him to play only with those things because

they're boy toys. In my opinion, when we make (speaks angrily) this gendered division of 'dolls are for girls' and 'cars are for boys,' we're already doing harm to the child. We all are. I think people should be exposed to everything, and only then, after being exposed to everything, we can choose what's good for us: "I like dolls more," "I like cars more," "I prefer to wear a necklace," or "I like to walk around with a hammer in my pocket." It doesn't matter. They must be exposed... I want to expose Andrew to everything, and present all the available options to him, and then for him to choose what is best for him, what fits him best. If he wants to play with Play-Doh, let him play with Play-Doh, and if he wants to do a puzzle, do a puzzle, read a book, play with dolls, cars, it doesn't matter, he needs to know everything and be exposed to everything. And then, I think, then, he'll always have the tools to choose correctly from all the options that will come his way throughout his life, not just now – to decide whether he plays with a doll or a car... In the future, it will be if he goes to study this or that profession and what he does with his money and what job he goes for... They're general tools for life. And I think gender division is wrong. It's not true for any family. When Andrew plays with my nieces and they dress up, if he chooses to wear a dress and walk around in it, then he should wear a dress and walk around in it, I have no problem with that. There's nothing wrong with it, and there's nothing inappropriate about it. I don't think it's bad, the opposite, role-playing games just help strengthen their development. Even when he understands that there's nothing right or wrong about his behavior, like, that it's not a matter of it being better to play with cars or worse... it will also give him more confidence to do the things he really loves to do. And it will give him the tools to always be confident in what he does.

Similarly, Sarah shared that she lets her daughter experiment with different games, roles, and gender-based activities, whether it's building, assembling, and disassembling with a "Bob the Builder" tool bag, hammers and sticks, or make-believe games with dolls. At the same time, she dresses her in dresses and pink clothes but also in her nephew's clothes. What's important to her is to show her daughter all the possibilities in a colorful and diverse world, so that she can make the decisions that most authentically and reliably reflect her wishes and preferences:

> *I give Nofar whatever she chooses, she has a Bob the Builder's tool bag, because she's very, very technical, she likes to take things apart and put them back together... So she can sit for hours doing that. But, she also has dolls, and she plays a lot with dolls, and plays make-believe. And she also has... we got clothes from my girlfriends, so most of them are, like, pink and purple, and we dress her in pink and purple, and she really likes dresses, so we dress her in dresses. But we also got clothes from my nephew, which are very, like, boyish, they're boys' clothes and I dress her up in boys' clothes, too. And actually, I'll just go along with whatever Naomi likes, what she finds fun. If she likes dresses, then I'll dress her up in dresses, and if she likes the color pink, I know, it's because other girls put it in her head, then I'll dress her in pink. And if she likes to build things and use hammers and nails, and she really does like that, she can spend hours outside. I let her... knock nails and hammers, and she likes taking sticks and playing with them. She's very technical, very, very technical. Moms who think that girls should be exposed to pink in order to develop the gender thing, for them to know that they are girls, seems to me to be also some kind of missed opportunity, because for me, in my opinion,*

it's all about the type of person. If the person is accepting and inclusive and knows and wants to show their child a colorful, diverse world in which all options are possible, they will let their child experience everything.

A minority of the narrators (8 out of 40, making up 20% of all the narrators) were involved in radical anti-sexist feminist education. They encouraged "plays" that involved blatant gender fluidity ("a boy will put on nail polish") both domestically and in public (on the street, in the kindergarten, at a pool). It was also important for them to educate their children to understand power relations in society. They described these practices in terms of a socio-political worldview, one that aims to undermine social power relations and propose alternatives to gender oppression.

Raya, for example, emphasized that she is a "feminist mother." According to her, her feminist motherhood manifests itself in raising her children's awareness as to the power relations inherent in society as well as anti-sexist education; her son walks around in public with ponytails and pink clothes. If it weren't for her partner's objections, she would dress him up in dresses in public:

I am a feminist mother. This means I try to think about the long term, about what kind of girl I'll have and what type of boy I'll have and what kind of adults they'll be. It means that I find it important to educate my children so they understand sexuality, understand violence, understand power, privilege... I also really love playing around with my children's genders. Especially with my son's, I mean... I make him pigtails, he wears pink often, even outside the house. Dresses – Nellie doesn't let, so no dresses, but if she didn't object, I would have been all for it...

The tendency of lesbian mothers in general, and feminist lesbi-an mothers in particular, to expose their children to a relatively wide range of gender roles, whether to address the children's developmental needs and promote their personal growth, or to challenge and offer alternatives to gender oppression in soci-ety, is documented in the theoretical and research literature.[44] Although no differences were observed between children from lesbian families and children from heterosexual ones on the development of gender identity and sexual orientation, chil-dren from lesbian families tended to be less strict about tradi-tional gender roles and more open about activities that don't identify with their gender. At the same time, girls felt they had more rights and boys were more nurturing than children from heterosexual families.[45] Children from lesbian families were also less likely to give credence to gender-stereotypical con-siderations when making decisions about careers and interests (Patterson, 1995).

It is important to note that all the narrators who addressed the issue of their children's sexual identity, both those who gave their children moderate exposure to a relatively wide range of gender roles and games, and those who were involved in a more radical anti-sexist feminist education, claimed that they would have no problem accepting a child with a different sexual ori-entation, but added that according to their impressions, their children are not gay or lesbian (and certainly not transgender). The pressure on narrators to raise their children with normative gender identities and sexual orientations is detailed in the next chapter about the complementary self-portrait.

In addition, many of the narrators claimed that they pro-mote values of openness, tolerance, acceptance of those who are

---

44. O'Reilly, 2004, 2008; Wells, 2001.

45. MacCallum and Golombok, 2004; Pridmore-Brown, 2008; Wells, 2001.

different, and helping the weak, to their children. They "branded" themselves and their "work as a mother" as role models of "value education."

Echoes of the notion that lesbian women encourage their children to be open and tolerant, can be found in research literature and public discourse. Lesbian mothers tend to be portrayed in public as developing an understanding and openness to diversity among their children.[46]

The link between same-sex mothers and educating on values of openness and tolerance, can be gleaned from Nora's words. In Nora's opinion, a lesbian mother will definitely educate her children to be more inclusive and tolerant of the different and the other, compared to a straight mother: "I think that lesbian mothers know how to educate their children to accept the different, the other, to be more inclusive, more patient. Definitely! lesbian mothers raise very special children! without a doubt!"

Ramona (a biological mother of a 10-year-old girl and 6-year-old boy in her mid-40s) noted that because she is different, she educates her children with universal humanistic values, such as loving all people and respecting those who are different:

In recent years, I've been realizing it more and more, and I, you know, it's starting to trickle down to the kids, as well. Meaning, I feel the moral role that I have. This is reflected in more general issues, not necessarily in lesbianism, but in instilling values about people's diversity and respecting people who are different and other people's choices. That is, to love a person, to respect people. To love the job too.

---

46. Clarke, 2002; Clarke and Kitzinger, 2004.

Sharon noted that she and her partner felt the need to instill in their children the message that "different is okay," also beyond the family context, and she uses TV shows that show children with disabilities so they can discuss the meaning of diversity and possible coping mechanisms:

> *Our approach with the kids was that being different is okay and that otherness is okay. And on the contrary, sometimes it's as if I, in my approach like to be something else. Like, I'm trying to trickle it down to them, and actually not through constantly chewing on the subject of our family, because I feel so normative. I don't have, I don't have the need to dwell on it and tell it to them all the time. But yes, just for example, we can watch a TV show about a disabled kid or a fat kid or just something out of the ordinary and talk with them about how wonderfully he copes with it and how okay it is, being fat is okay and being dark-skinned is okay, and things like that.*

Audrey (a non-biological mother of a 7-year-old girl and 5-year-old girl in her early 40s) emphasized that she has a moral educational role when it comes to raising her children's awareness of minorities and equal rights:

> *I think that in our home the topic of minorities, no matter what kind of minority, a national minority or something else, is much more prominent than in ordinary families. Because you can't demand equal rights for us and not give it to another minority, that wouldn't make any sense at all. But it takes effort, to see who the minority is, in what situation, and which... To see what equality actually is, what it means in practice. What I have to do for it. I do see*

that we have some educational and moral role that I don't
see in everyone.

Finally, the narrators claimed that they foster resistance and
negotiation skills in their children, and encourage them to ask
questions and think critically. Gaia argued that it's important
for her to equip her daughter with tools that will help her cope
with life in the best possible way. Accordingly, she educates her
to accept authority, on the one hand, but also to confront her
and her partner from time to time on the other:

I want to give her all the tools for her to manage in the
world. Um, so she'll know how to accept authority because,
bottom line, it makes life easier. Um, knowing how to
accept authority, but not at all costs! I also like when she
locks horns with us sometimes... As exhausting as it can be
in the moment – overall, it's wonderful! so, so there's that.
What is important to me, I make sure to emphasize.

Audrey also noted that she and her partner educate their daughters to ask critical questions, to free themselves from social dic-
tates, and to increase their range of options, in contrast to heterosexual mothers who are busy preserving and transcripting
the conservative social reality:

I, as well as my partner, have a much more liberating
approach to education than I see among most heterosexuals
around. And on purpose. We decided that we needed
to raise children, inspire them to ask questions and get
answers, increase the range, increase the possibilities of
what can be done in life. I see many of our girlfriends who
are married to men accepting the reality. That's just how it

is. That's just how it is. That's just... They don't even try to build different relationships with their husbands, they're not trying to make social change. They simply continue what they learned at home, when they were kids. There is no change in this generation and it drives me crazy!

Chapter 5

LESBIAN MOTHERHOOD
UNDER THE BURDEN OF PROOF

A complementary self-portrait

In their public-representative self-portrait, the narrators produced a representative version of themselves, sort of a "narrative identity card ," to present to the world, in which they describe themselves as normal, valuable women and worthy mothers. However, an analysis of the narrators' statements showed that the public-representative self-portrait presented a partial and selective aspect of the narrators' identities. Alongside the public-representative self-portrait, a "complementary self-portrait" was revealed. In this complementary self-portrait, other voices emerged, which were silenced or only partially expressed in their self-presentation, because they did not conform to the central identity claims that the representative narrative tried to promote. These voices expressed unique hardships, dilemmas, fears, and challenges.

This distinction between a "public-representative self-portrait" and a "complementary self-portrait" is based on ideas put forth by narrative theorists who discuss the relationship between 'self' and identity (Spector-Mersel, 2011, 2012). De Medeiros (2005) describes two "selves" which exist side by side, and are negotiated by the narrators and their audience: The "externally presented self" and the "complementary self." The "externally presented self" expresses the narrator's attempt to create an ideal self, while the "complementary self" represents more private aspects, such as thoughts, feelings, and aspirations, that are liable to conflict with social norms and therefore are not represented in the representative narrative.

This chapter presents the difficulties, stressors, and challenges faced by the narrators and their children, as reflected in the analysis of their narratives. These difficulties and challenges include having to be vigilant, manage information, and stand guard in the face of the hostile world, the psychological pressure of being a shining example of normalcy and excellence to prove their value as mothers ("the burden of proof"), trial and error, biological inequality and internalized homophobia in the couple's relationship, concern about the effects of sexual orientation and fatherlessness, and the pressure to raise "straight" children, the increased stress experienced by children ("affiliate stigma") and the dialogue challenges with them, institutionalized discrimination and the socioeconomic disadvantage, as well as coping with incidents of rejection, violence, and discrimination stemming from both families of origin and the medical, educational, and social environment.

Vigilance, information management, and standing guard against a hostile world

Careful listening to the narratives, following The Listening Guide: A voice-centered relational method,[47] exposed the emotional experience of the narrators as based on lack of protection and vulnerability. This lack of protection is reflected, first and

---

47. Gilligan and Eddy, 2017; Gilligan, et al., 2003

foremost, in the narrators' probability to serve as a target for hostile and abusive reactions from families of origin and their social environment (peers in class, other children's parents, neighborhood youth, etc.). This expectation was not centered on the one major event of "coming out," but accompanied the narrators through various stages of same-sex family development. It was sometimes conscious and sometimes not. In some cases, the expectation of being harmed was undue, while in others it was justified. However, whether the expectation/worry? of being harmed was actually fulfilled or not, it led to tension and emotional stress among the narrators, to hypervigilance and alertness, and defensive and non-adaptive responses.

We learn from the narrators' reports that the experience of insecurity and vulnerability was largely influenced by a social and political landscape, rife with violence, stress around physical and economic security, and homophobia. Homophobic slurs frequently uttered by youth in the neighborhood or in public parks, creating an overall intolerant atmosphere, and the growing conservative and anti-democratic religious movements and political trends in society, formed rifts and shook many of the narrators' sense of security.

Toby shared her concerns about moving the girls to new kindergartens near their homes at the beginning of the school year. She expressed worry that her daughters would be exposed to offensive remarks from other kindergarten children and their parents, and would come home with feedback such as: "Mom, they told us that you're perverts and gross, and that people hate you and all sorts of things, that it's against the Torah," given that the neighborhood they are in is mostly populated by religious residents who vote for an ultra-Orthodox party. The "enormous fear" of offensive reactions, coupled with the general anxiety about the uncertainty, cause her to straddle the tension between two opposite extremes: An attempt to repress thoughts about the beginning of the school year ("I don't want to think about what's going to happen on September 1st"), and pressure, vigilance, and "readiness for battle," and planning possible combat strategies (appealing to the media, using connections to help them transfer the girls to another kindergarten).

Toby's repeated use of the metaphor and figurative language of "war" ("This is what there is and with this we will go to war," "We'll use all the tools at our disposal") illustrates the difficult psychological experience of having one's self-worth being threatened, and the need for the most basic conditions of security, protection, and belonging. Similar to post-traumatic (social) trauma, the trauma caused by actual injuries from the past, produces repression and an attempt to avoid stressful situations on the one hand, and to be vigilant and hypersensitive, and sometimes even to expect rejection and further harm (which sometimes plays out and sometimes doesn't), on the other:

The older girl is about to move to a municipal kindergarten near home. The neighborhood we live in is in the south of the city, um... the residents there vote for Shas, they're Bukharan, they're not really open people... But, again, there's the neighborhood community center where we do go, and when we're there, we don't hide. And we explain that we are a family, that we are together. So it's well-accepted at the community center, there are those, of course, who have reservations... I really hope that... With the start of the school year in both Nadine and Melanie's kindergartens, we come as one unit, we come as a family, "If you want to accept it – do, if you don't want to – don't." If it will be very, very bad and horrible, we'll act accordingly... We won't stay at this kindergarten. You know, like if there'll be, I don't know, I won't tell you protests and all that, but if we feel like crap and the girls come home with words like,

"Mom, they told us that you're perverts and gross, and that people hate you and all sorts of things, that it's against the Torah," stuff like that. Because in my head, you know, I'm going crazy in all directions, I don't know what's going to happen. I'm terribly afraid, the fear is enormous, because, because, both the fear of the unknown and also because of what we do know, it's not, oh my goodness. So we're like 'at the ready,' you know, this is what there is, and with this we will go to war. I hope it won't be a war, I don't want it to be a war, because we see the goodness of our children before our eyes. This... in all honesty, cross my heart, you know, I'm talking to you about a concern that is current. When it was July, the month of July, so I told Zara [my partner, A.P.] "Oh no, the next school year." So she says to me, "Babe, what do you mean 'next school year'?! It's in a second from now, like three weeks or a month away." And I told her, "I must be repressing it deep down... Oh, it's a long way away, a long time from now, it's only the end of July now." I told her, " Okay, I don't want to think about what's going to happen on September 1st." I hope it will be good, I really hope that we'll do everything possible for it to be good. And if it's not, we'll turn to the media. I told her, we talked about everything, we'll go to the media, we'll cause a stir, we'll talk, anything we can do. If necessary, we'll also make sure to use connections and transfer them to another kindergarten. My brother told me that he knows some people in the municipality, I said: "Hopefully we won't need to," but, if, God forbid, if we need to, and ... we'll use all the tools at our disposal. There's the media, there's Amnon Levy [journalist, A.P.], and today, you know, people who will be very happy... to say, "Hey, hey, there's discrimination here, there's everything." I really hope we don't have to, and that it won't come to this...

Jessie (a non-biological mother of a 5-year-old girl and 3-year-old girl in her late 30s) spoke about "fear" as a formative experience in her emotional world and in her relationship with Israeli society. In addition to the economic and security stressors, she highlighted intolerance and homophobia as sources of insecurity and lack of protection for her and her daughters, as well as the strengthening of conservative and religious elements, while more liberal elements are falling to the wayside. She says that although there is a lot of public discourse on the subject, the frequent homophobic curses she can hear children utter in her yard, prove to her that most parents do not fight homophobia or educate their children to be tolerant. In addition, the feminist struggle did not reach a satisfactory level of fulfillment, and the strengthening religious and conservative forces have not been stifled by the insufficiently strong liberal ones. Given this socio-political climate, she fears that her daughters will have to deal with a difficult reality:

> *I have many concerns... I'm full of concerns about our country's economic situation, I'm full of concerns about the girls' lives. What will be, how it will be. It's scary here. It's really scary here. I can't say that I feel that the children of our generation are more advanced than we were. I hear children down here, every other word – "You're so gay, you're so gay." It's the same. Because, as mentioned, most of the straight parents are the same. And if they don't make a difference in their children's lives, there won't be a difference in my children's lives. They will be living in the same world. On the one hand, there's a lot of externalization of the issue and a lot of, you see it coming up a lot in discourse and a lot in schools... and also, supposedly, as part of the feminist umbrella. But I feel, and I am generally an optimistic person, that*

our movement and our struggle have not been fulfilled and are not strong enough. And that's why I somehow think that my daughters will have to deal with an equally difficult reality. It scares me a lot. Society. Society scares me. The strengthening religious side, the fact that there isn't a strong enough alternative being offered to the strengthening of the religious, no driving force of liberalism, humanism, pluralism. All the fundamentalist forces that are getting stronger, they will continue to grow stronger. I'm afraid of it. Less afraid of national security threats. That's also scary. Basically, I'm full of concerns.

"Anticipated stigma," "perceived stigma," or "felt stigma," is mentioned in the research and theoretical literature as one of the primary stressors faced by people with stigmatized identity.[48] Meyer (1995, 2003) described "expectations of rejection and discrimination" as a prominent component of "minority stress" experienced by homosexuals, lesbians, and bisexuals. According to him, whether this expectation is fulfilled or not, the expectation itself can be a source of stress, anxiety, and mental illness. Affirmations of this claim can be found in various studies. Quinn and Chaudoir (2009) examined 300 participants in the United States with concealable stigmatized identities (such as different sexual orientation, epilepsy, AIDS, and mental illness) and found that "anticipated stigma" tends to be a powerful predictor for mental well-being and physical health. That is, the more a person believes that others would devalue and harm them if they knew about their identity, the more likely they are to suffer psychological distress and symptoms of physical illness. Ross (1985), in cross-cultural research among homosexual individuals,

---

48. Allport, 1954; Goffman, 1963; Meyer, 1995, 2003; Quinn and Chaudoir, 2009; Ross, 1985.

found that expectations of social exclusion predicted psychological distress to a greater extent than actual negative experiences.

"Perceived stigma" has also been found to have a significant impact on the lives of mothers in planned lesbian families. Boss et al., (2004) shows that lesbian mothers in the Netherlands that showed higher degrees of anticipated stigma, felt the need to justify and defend their position as mothers more often than lesbian mothers that showed lower degrees of anticipated stigma. Meir (2008) found that lesbian mothers (single and coupled) and single heterosexual mothers in Israel expected to endure experiences of rejection, violence, and discrimination more than heterosexual coupled mothers. The level of anticipation predicted their level of psychological distress and parental stress, that is, the higher their expectation of experiences of rejection and discrimination, the more likely they were to experience symptoms of psychological distress and parental stress.

Multiple readings of the narratives have shown that the fundamental experience of a lack of protection and the expectation of experiencing harm, greatly shaped the narrators' attitude toward the world and influenced their interactions with those around them. Along with adopting a psychological-cognitive-behavioral stance of hypervigilance and constant alertness, the narrators were largely concerned with managing information around their sexual orientation and family differences. Each transition from one framework to another (moving to a new house, moving to a new job, transferring the children to new educational frameworks) and every encounter with new people (neighbors, colleagues, teachers, friends of the children), was a stressful event and required the narrators to deal with questions of what to share, what not to share, whom to share with, when is the right time to share, etc., while assessing prospects and risks around what exposure would mean and what consequences it would have. Sometimes, they had to do "advocacy work" after being exposed and advocate for themselves.

According to Jessie, being constantly preoccupied with managing information about their sexual orientation and family differences, is one of the main differences in motherhood between lesbian women and heterosexual women. Unlike mothers in heterosexual families, mothers in same-sex families have to introduce themselves and their families whenever they meet new people, such as the parents in the new classroom, and explain themselves. Any such exposure is accompanied by emotional stress and fear of others' reactions:

> *Mothers in straight families have a different job in that they don't have to constantly present themselves to groups of people that are related to the children, that are not related to the children, that are related to both the children and the family. There isn't this whole dimension of being different. Meaning... of leading a different life, which the vast majority of people aren't familiar with, and at least half of which reject it all, this kind of life. They don't have this tension every time at the beginning of every school year when you talk to the other parents – "Are they cool?!, are they not cool?!, will they accept it?!, how will the girls get along?!" =they don't need to deal with all that. Again, this is a rough generalization of all straight people. We're not talking about families with, I don't know, any disabilities or special children.*

Toby described the experience of "coming out" as a formative and ongoing experience in her life, one that she is required to do time and time again in different situations and at different points in time (job interview, girls' entry into a new educational framework). Exposing sexual orientation and family diversity often arouses curiosity, unpleasant comments, and intrusive questions from those around her, and she is forced to carry out advocacy work and self-defense. The emotional stress and mental strain involved in coping with the excited, intrusive, and hurtful reactions, cause her to be picky about the situations and people she reveals her intimate life to:

> *"Coming out of the closet" is not "coming out of the closet," and that's it. You know, people talk about, "When did you come out of the closet?" and say the date, "Yes, I was here, I was there." But, every day, we "come out of the closet" all over again... It's not like I feel like I have to "come out" to every X and Y I meet on the street, or that provides some kind of service. But there are times when I don't give a damn, and say, "I don't have to, I don't know them, and I won't see them again for years, or at all." Gal Uchovsky [an openly gay TV personality, A.P.] once said, "Every time I meet an old acquaintance or friend, I come out again." And that's true, actually, in our day-to-day. Like now, we're going to "come out" at the kids' new kindergartens. I came here for an interview about a year or so ago, I "came out of the closet." When I "came out" at another job interview, the curiosity, you know, people get really curious, "Oh, do you live with a female partner?! Do you have children?" And here and there, there are those who are a bit nosy. But, yes, we "come out" all the time... it's kind of... you're developing some kind of routine where you know you need to introduce yourself to and that's you. It would be much easier if I say, "My husband." We just booked a vacation, something modest, in August, and the owner of the place said to me, "You and your husband." You know, I didn't bother correcting her. And people look right away, "Yeah, but this girl looks like you and this*

*girl looks like you, and she's like this and she's like that,"
"What really?!" There are some people who show courage
and ask, "And who's the man in the house, which one
of you?" My cosmetologist, the one I go to for a monthly
pluck said, "Can I ask you a question?" "Yes." "How are
you managing with your bank account?" "Can I ask you
a question? They say there's a man and there's a woman,
so how...?" So, it's like that... yes, we're constantly "coming
out of the closet," constantly explaining...*

Zara "distilled" the essence of her, her partner's, and their
daughters' lives in terms of "struggle," amidst the need to share
their sexual orientation and family differences ("coming out of
the closet"), and being exposed over and over again to potential
torment and harassment by those around her. According to her,
this fear of being potentially harmed makes them constantly remain in an alert state ("You must always be aware, constantly be
paying attention"):

*Look, the very fact that we live this way is a struggle. It's
already a struggle. That you have to "come out" at school
all the time, again and again, and another one finds out
and another one finds out. And when they [the kids, A.P.]
grow up, it gets harder. They're small now, so they're
still small children, they don't quite understand that you
can get hurt through this, too. When they get older, then
they'll understand that you can get hurt from this, too.
Then they will start using it, the children around them.
And then it will start to be a different kind of coping. Um...
that's it, so it really is a struggle. This way of life itself is a
struggle, and you must always be, I think, aware. I mean,
constantly be paying attention...*

The constant need to manage information and the dilemma of whether to reveal or conceal information about your diversity, all while handling an invisible stigma, are described in the research and theoretical literature as an additional aspect of stress among minority groups.[49] "Concealment" is a prominent component of the "minority stress" model presented by Meyer (1995, 2003). According to him, lesbians, homosexuals, and bisexuals tend to hide their sexual orientation to protect themselves from real harm (such as violence, or losing their job) or alternatively, out of shame and guilt.

A comparative study in the United States (DeMino, et al., 2007) showed that mothers in planned lesbian families reported a higher degree of stress and anxiety around issues of managing information and disclosing sexual orientation, compared to lesbian women who were not mothers. The researchers conclude that for lesbian mothers, selective disclosure of their sexual orientation can reflect an attempt to protect their children from social stigma.

Keeping secrets, however, is a heavy mental burden and may harm the mental well-being and physical health of individuals with same-sex orientation (Meyer, 1995, 2003). Concealing one's stigma can have cognitive, emotional, and behavioral consequences. When it comes to cognition, concealing a stigma can lead to excessive worrying, vigilance, and suspicion. Regarding emotions, it can provoke anxiety, depression, hostility, guilt and shame, and have a negative impact on a person's self-esteem. Regarding behavior, it can be expressed in an increase in self-criticism and impression management, social avoidance, and isolation (Pachankis, 2007).

We can see from the narrators' words that the dilemma of

---

49. Shilo, 2007 [Hebrew]; Quinn and Chaudoir, 2009; Pachankis, 2007; Beals, et al., 2009.

whether or not to reveal their sexual orientation and family differences was not where their preoccupation with information management ended. The narrators were busy protecting their stance and juggling the different aspects of information and impression management, even after coming out. These aspects included putting on a "common front" against a "hostile world ," overprotection of children, preparing children and equipping them with a pail of responses, silencing weaknesses and difficulties and avoiding asking for help.

Toby described her life in terms of an "emergency routine" that required her to be in "constant, routine, existential, and daily level of preparedness" and sometimes even "go to war" against the doubts, questions, and ponderings of families of origin and the surroundings. Since, in her view, people are just waiting for same-sex families to "slip up," to "taunt" her and her partner, rebuke them for their "wrong choice" or try to sabotage her, she and her partner take special protective measures such as demonstrating a "strong united front" to the outside world:

> *Our families – as accepting and everything as they are – as far as the families are concerned... there are times when my mom can say, "My Melanie," um... "her Nadine" ... It's not as simple as it seems and is. Um... we decided that we would show a common front, no cracks, no slip-ups, so that no one could take advantage of the cracks and slip-ups, to attack us or create, all sorts of, you know, doubts of one kind or another. Because it exists! people are just waiting, you know, one leg crossed over the other, sitting suddenly, boom start talking your ear off about what's not right, deciding what it was that went wrong, "Our way is better for you," and all kinds of stuff like that... and with all this going on, we make sure to present, once again, a type of façade so that even if it's not okay, everything's okay,*

more or less... Because, again, it creates space, especially if there are doubts and questions, here, it's time to jam the stick in the wheels, and make it, I don't know what. It's not always like this, but, it exists, again I'm telling you, it's in the back of your head, it's there. So yes, unlike the relationships of a typical straight woman and her friends, um... we're in some type of constant, routine, existential, daily level of preparedness that... this is our lifestyle, this is what we chose, this is what we will deal with, with this we'll go to war or to work, or whatever you want to call it...

Echoes of the need to convey a message that "everything is fine" and that "there's no problem" can also be found in Tara's words. Tara (a biological mother of a 4-year-old girl and a 1-year-old baby boy in her late 30s) mentioned the importance of conveying that "everything is fine" and that there is "nothing out of the ordinary" to the socio-educational environment, so as not to give ammunition to the people who want to label her and her partner as non-normative and their daughter, Bailey, as abnormal:

I'm not saying there won't be hardships, and I'm not saying there won't be any... you know, you have to give off the impression that everything is fine, that everything is normal, that everything is normative, and everything is fine. So if you give it off, then it's all okay. In first grade, you buy a book by Yehuda Atlas, "Everyone and His Family," for the whole class and that's it (laughs), a birthday present for the whole class and that's it (laughs). And then they know... you have to convey that everything is fine, that there is nothing out of the ordinary, to everyone who doubts you, to everyone who wants to label you, to everyone who... implies that it's... that you're not normative, that Bailey is different, that Bailey is abnormal. This means

> *that no one will come and say to Bailey, "you're abnormal*
> *because you have a mother and a mommy."*

The expectation of harm, or alternatively, previous experiences of actual incidents of harm, led some of the narrators to become defensive and overprotective of their children. Heidi stressed her reputation as a "crazy bulldozer," a "crazy mom," and "that masculine lesbian who threatens children at school," as a result of her aggressive behavior when it comes to those who harm her children:

> *I'm known as a crazy bulldozer, but like, crazy. A tiger is*
> *small compared to me when people touch my children.*
> *Sometimes it reaches levels of madness, so people know*
> *not to go near Johnny and Tanya, they don't come close.*
> *If you were to talk to Johnny, he would say, "Mama Heidi*
> *is the toughest mom in school," that's how he would say*
> *it, "she's the strongest." Why the "toughest?" because*
> *when someone messes with him, I go straight to the child,*
> *I don't turn to the parents at all, I don't go through the*
> *parents, because some parents don't even listen at all.*
> *I'm completely direct. I don't care what they say, on the*
> *contrary, I portray, as I've said, a very aggressive woman*
> *and also certainly that "masculine lesbian who threatens*
> *children at school," and it doesn't matter to me, I'm that*
> *"masculine threatening lesbian," that "crazy one," but no*
> *one will come close to my child, compared to other mothers*
> *who are straight.*

At the end of the interview, Heidi explained her need to communicate power, strength, and aggression to the external environment as a defense and compensation mechanism that she had built for herself over many years to survive and avoid being hurt.

Johnny and Tanya see me as something very powerful, very mighty. Society also sees me as something very powerful and mighty. And that often drives people away because they're terrified by the tons of self-confidence that isn't actually there. There is self-confidence, but not tons of it as the outside perceives, it's there but not at such a crazy level. I give off a lot of aggression, a lot of force, aggression and force. But, those are two things I'm not. I'm not aggressive at all, I'm really not aggressive. They're defenses, of the years, of life, of having no choice, of I have no choice. When you live in secret all your life until the age of 32, you have no choice. I lived in secret until age 32. How do we define it? I lived in my socks, in the socks drawer, in the drawer inside the closet. That's how much I was in the closet. Olivia, my partner, would leave the house: "Olivia, did someone see you, did any of the neighbors see you leave?" she would leave with her head down so they wouldn't see her. We would leave on opposite sides of the yard, I was really scared to death. So this is someone with tons of confidence and strength?! nope. But you build up over the years because there's no choice. So that they won't hurt me. Because I was hurt so much.

Daria's words also display hypervigilance, sensitivity, and over-protection when she recently felt unsafe leaving her son alone, even with her parents and sister. She described her motherhood before the outside world and families of origin (representatives of the hostile heteronormative and heterosexist order) as a "guard" equipped with sharp, violent, and murderous weapons ("you're with knives and you have to protect"), who is constantly on guard to protect her son and family from homophobic and racist statements, and expressions of violence. If necessary, she uses violence against violence. In fact, apart from her home, it seems that every other space – her parents' house, the pool, the street, etc. – is experienced as a potential threatening space of violence and unwanted influences, and she finds herself in an ongoing and endless battle with her surroundings for control and influence over the consciousness, values, and choices of her current child and her future children:

From the moment you don't tell your child he's different, then he's not different. And if someone, if I catch someone around who just dares, you know, I straighten things out right away, I don't wait, I straighten things out gently, and sometimes not so gently... I'm very... let's say that I don't leave him alone around my parents or sister. If I do, it's just these days, when I know he's a bit more stable but before... I wouldn't leave him. And even today, I'm always alert. Even if he's with her parents and with that person, I'm all the time... I'll talk to someone, I'll be alert, I'll hear about what's going to go down, what's going on. For the reason that if someone out of the ordinary happens, I can respond... These days, I'm no longer afraid because I know he already has his opinions and that he is already a pretty developed kid, but a year ago, for sure I was afraid that, you know, someone will just come up to him and say, and suppose I'm not around, and they'll say to him... "Gay," or I don't know, anything, it's bad. People are dumb, they don't think there's a child here. So that's... That's the thing I was most afraid of. Now it begins to relax. And I'm alert even now, I will always be alert. Yes, there's nothing to do, for example, I will never tell him: "This is an Arab, this is a Jew, this is ... I don't know what." Because they're a human being, it doesn't matter. He knows: there are people who speak Arabic, there are people who speak Hebrew, there are people who speak Russian, there are... I don't bring up those differences to him. I don't want to instill this racism in him from a young age. I don't want to. So he's a little bit, he's already a bit more shaped, you know. Now there will be another child and another child, everyone has to be shaped, there is nothing we can do. To protect, yes, you feel like you're with knives and you need to protect. That you need to protect, to be alert all the time. In front of people.

Some of the narrators reported that they prepare their children for unpleasant questions and situations, and equip them with an appropriate "box of answers." Sharon said that she doesn't remember a time when the children raised questions or concerns about their family differences or the fact that they didn't have a father, "because it's normal for them." That being said, she and her partner felt compelled to equip them with a box of answers nonetheless:

I don't remember when it started but um... first of all it didn't come up from them. Okay? I don't think I've ever experienced a question, I'm trying to remember, of "Mom, why are we different?" or "Why are we a family like this?" or I've never encountered a question like "Why don't I have a father?" it's something that looks, I think, like when I look at them, like it's natural. Sherry and I felt the need, it didn't come from them, we felt the need to equip them with the tools of what is called a box of answers, or to explain to them the correct status, or how it can look to others. Let's say there are people who can look at you as something different. But the attitude was that being different is okay and that something different is okay.

Tara emphasized how important it is for her to convey to her daughters that they are not abnormal ("freak show"), to prepare

them ahead of time for comments and teasing, and to strength-
en their resilience and confidence:

> *Now this is what I always say, and in general, that what*
> *you give off to the child is what the child will be... it's*
> *important for us to give the girls the sense that everything*
> *is okay, and that they're, as a family unit, not some kind of*
> *freak show, they're nothing abnormal. They should have*
> *the resilience, the confidence! when children tease them*
> *later on and tell them, "You don't have a father," which*
> *is probably what they'll do... they'll come at them and tell*
> *them things and attack... the kids will... so the girls should*
> *know how to say, "No, it's okay, there's no problem with*
> *that, it's fine, it's totally fine, there's nothing shameful*
> *about it, it's not embarrassing." They need to be prepared.*
> *I think they need to be strong enough to be able to respond*
> *on their own. When we're with them, of course there's no*
> *problem. The trick is what will happen when she's in 2nd*
> *and 3rd grade, and 4th, and 5th, and 6th, where she will*
> *have to answer on her own.*

The narrators' accounts help us understand that their need to
demonstrate a united front and to constantly be giving off the
impression that "everything is fine," is often accompanied by
the self-silencing of weaknesses and difficulties, and refraining from asking for help. For example, when Toby discussed
how she and her partner decided to present a common front
to the outside world, in the same breath she emphasized how
it was impossible to show weaknesses. Later in her interview,
she clarified that even if they face difficulties, they make sure
to present a semblance of "everything being fine." "We decided
that we would show a common front, no cracks, no slip ups... We
make sure to present a type of façade so that even if it's not okay,

everything's okay, more or less..." From such situations, we can assume that their ability to inspire empathy or seek help, and support from families of origin and the socio-educational environment on an ongoing basis, is quite limited.

Confirmations and reverberations of the hypervigilance, alertness, and defensive coping mechanisms among people suffering from stigmas can be found in the theoretical and research literature on the topic of stigmas. Goffman (1963) discusses the anxiety with which a person, carrying the burden of stigma, approaches interactions in society. Someone like that might think (often rightly so) that no matter what others declare, they won't actually "accept" him, and they won't be willing to communicate with him on an equal basis.

Allport (1954) described vigilance as one of the traits that people who are objects of prejudice, develop in defensive coping. People belonging to minorities who suffer from a negative social label, learn to expect negative treatment from members of the dominant group. In order to monitor potential negative attitudes, discrimination, or violence, they must remain vigilant. The higher the expectation of a person from a minority group to experience harm, the greater the need for vigilance in interactions with members of the dominant group. By definition, vigilance appears to be chronic in the daily life of the stigmatized person in a repeated manner.

The relationship between the experience of minority stress among mothers in planned same-sex families and parental protection, can be gleaned from the study by Boss et al., (2004). Mothers in planned same-sex families in the Netherlands who suffered a large number of rejection incidents and reported high degrees of anticipated stigma and internalized homophobia, felt the need to defend their maternal position and justify the quality of their parenting to the social environment to a greater extent.

Psychological Pressure to Be a Shining Example of Normalcy and Excellence (the 'Burden of Proof')

The narrators in this book started building their families from the 1990s onwards, thus constituting the "first generation" of mothers in planned lesbian families in Israel. At the end of each interview, they were asked to consider the historical context of their families' primary position and try to gauge the impact that their pioneering location has on their emotional experiences, conduct, and motherhood. The narrators were divided into three "waves": Narrators whose first child was born between 1995–1999 were associated with the "first wave," narrators who made the transition to motherhood between 2000–2009 were part of the "second wave,' while narrators whose first child was born between 2010–2016 were part of the "third wave."

The narrators who began building their families in the 1990s, and who were part of the "first wave" generation, tended to speak of a very heavy burden on their shoulders, often consciously and often less so, to serve as models of normalcy and excellence, to "prove" to themselves and to heterosexual society that they are competent women and worthy mothers. I called this **"The burden of proof"** (Peleg & Hartman, 2019). However, this "burden of proof" motif was not exclusive to the "first wave" narrators. It came up again, to varying degrees, in the tales of some of the "second wave" and "third wave" mothers, who built their families from the year 2000 onwards.

Gabriella (a biological mother of a 17-year-old girl and a non-biological mother of a 12-year-old girl in her late 40s), who is part of the "first wave" first generation, referred to the historical-cultural significance of this "breakthrough," in that it was a "very heavy burden." From her perspective, this pioneering status set her out to justify the task she had undertaken, and prove that she was an ideal, unrivaled mother, and that her children were the most unique and successful. Unlike heterosexual mothers, who can enjoy the (relative) privilege of being "good enough mothers" (Winnicott, 1973) and the (relative) freedom to raise children through trial and error, through making mistakes and correcting them, Gabriella felt that she couldn't afford to be a "good enough wife/friend/mother" ("You can't be good enough at anything"), function at a mediocre level or make mistakes ("There's no room here for mediocrity, no room for "almost," and no room for "maybe"). Much of her consciousness, conduct, and work as a mother are shaped by a very strong need, which in retrospect is mostly "primal and unconscious," to get people to acknowledge her quality, excellence, and effectiveness as a mother in a same-sex family:

> *Being first matters. It matters because you can't be good enough at anything. You have to be the absolute best and justify your existence. "You decided to be a trailblazer?!" "You want to start a family with your female partner and have children?!" "Come show us that you're not like the other mothers, that your children are the most magical thing on earth, and that you are the most valuable mother you can be, something really original." And the burden of proof is on you! there's no room here for mediocrity, no room for "almost," and no room for "maybe." And it's a very, very heavy burden. And I feel it a lot of the time. Look, I also have a bit of an urge in my personality to be the ultimate best... but we have a very big need, one that, in retrospect, is completely primal and unconscious, to be... the best. So that you see my children and say, "Wow, they're incredible. What amazing children you have, what good education, what a nice home!"*

Later on, Gabriella came to the conclusion that motherhood has, to a large extent, become some type of "work" ("you work in it"), where she needs to invest time, attention, and resources, to specialize in it, become an expert and excel in. With the absence of previous models of planned fatherless same-sex families in Israel, her need to "work in motherhood" stemmed from her self-doubt and her desire to prove – first and foremost to herself and then to others – that her choice to raise children in a fatherless same-sex family, is the right, responsible, and appropriate choice:

> *The one side of this is that it's exhausting and there isn't...*
> *you can't just let things go. The other side of this, I think*
> *it takes us to a place... where you work in it. Meaning,*
> *I think a lot of people look and say, "I think we made a*
> *mistake with the kid when we did that" or "I think that*
> *that's not enough." But I didn't even have the privilege of*
> *saying that, because we worked in it. And at the end of*
> *the day, we put a lot of attention into it so that it would*
> *be right. So the girls don't have a father, so... you know,*
> *in order to prove... that is, it leads to even when you have*
> *to prove something to yourself, to be sure that you did the*
> *right thing, you work and invest in it. So that in the end*
> *you can say – here, we did the work and it worked!*

Similarly, Tiffany (a non-biological mother of a 19-year-old girl and a 14-year-old boy in her late 40s), a member of the "first wave," spoke of the constant need to demonstrate an ideal of health, normality, and efficiency ("You always have to be... as normal as normal can be") vis-à-vis heteronormative society, due to the need to prove that a same-sex family is a normal and proper family configuration, and that the children are healthy and successful. From her words, we can understand that the homogeneous heteronormative environment in which they live ("there wasn't one divorced family") only deepened and intensified the feeling of being different and the "burden of proof":

When it comes to being in front of... in front of the whole world, you always have to be, you always have to be more, like as normal as normal can be, because you're, like, trying to prove that your family is normal and your children are normative. That the attitude should be the same towards us, as though we are actually a family that's just like all the other families. And you don't want your children to suffer because they come from a different family. And maybe if we lived in Tel Aviv, which is... the environment there is a bit more diverse, so maybe in that respect it would have been easier. But in my eldest daughter Sammy's class, there wasn't one divorced family. So, she was, there were 39 children, each of whom had a mother and father. And then there was Sammy. A very, very homogeneous population. Then, like later on, over the years, it changed a little bit. So you always have to be this kind of perfect role model. So, also when it comes to... honestly, this is life in general. I think I feel this way with a lot of other things, too. It doesn't say anything about me, it says more, I think (smiles), about the people around me.

The impact of this pioneering, historical position and living in the shadow of the "burden of proof" in a heterosexual society, weren't just the yoke of first-generation "first-wave" women. They were also present on different levels of intensity in the narratives of "second-wave" and "third-wave" women. Adriana, a member of the second wave, reported that when it comes to families of origin, she is particularly strict about upholding the children's rules of conduct, as well as holding family ceremonies in the spirit of reform and feminist principles by which she educates her children. These family "performances" allow her to prove her competence in managing her family effectively, and

according to values that are important to her, before the scruti-
nizing and skeptical eyes of families of origin:

> *I sometimes feel like I have to prove myself because, for*
> *example, Hellen always tells me that I'm more radical when*
> *her family is around. I mean, when her family is around, I*
> *put greater emphasis on following our principles than usual.*
> *It's important for me to show that our family is functioning,*
> *that it has a certain shape, and that this is how things*
> *work. It can be about conduct, and it could be about um...*
> *suddenly I'll make more of a big deal about "welcoming the*
> *Sabbath" or I'll want to show that we do that, too. I don't do*
> *it all the time, but when they come, it's extra important for*
> *me. I have this thing that says, "Look at this, I'm a woman*
> *who does Kiddush and I'm a woman who... yeah." I have*
> *an urge to show that not only does a woman know, but that*
> *you can run a family like this, and that that's okay. Or I'll*
> *suddenly notice things I don't normally do. Like, if I take*
> *welcoming the Sabbath, then I usually don't care if the*
> *daughter does the Kiddush and the son lights the candles,*
> *or vice versa. But when the grandparents are around, that's*
> *when I specifically prefer that the son lights the candles and*
> *the daughter says Kiddush. It... leaves an impact.*

Audrey, a member of the "second wave," claimed that stress is
an issue all the time, but that it calmed down over the years.
On a personal and family level, she already feels like they have
passed all the tests, and that the burden of proof is behind them.
She looks at her daughters with satisfaction and pride and already sees that they are "much better than the mainstream." On
a social and political level, she feels that the mothers who are
over 50, were the trailblazers and that her main task is to reinforce the infrastructure:

Of course there's stress. Absolutely. It's a constant subject. Um... now that I see how much, how good mothers we are overall, I already feel less stressed. I see that our girls are much better than the mainstream (laughs), so we've already succeeded. We don't have to wait for 18 years to pass. I also don't feel like we're the first generation, I feel more like the second. The first generation, mothers today aged fifty and up, are the ones who broke through and did a lot of work. They took a lot of responsibility and success on themselves. I really feel more like the second generation that can now reinforce the infrastructure. I don't have to be a trailblazer. As far as I'm concerned. There are still political demands, but not at that level, as far as I'm concerned.

She went on to clarify and drive home that although she faces less of a "burden of proof" and a lower degree of stress, they are still present in her life and influence her behavior in various contexts. Thus, for example, while she feels comfortable walking around in pajamas in her own neighborhood, because "everyone knows that [they're] such good and smart mothers" (i.e., she and her partner have already proven themselves to be worthy mothers **in the neighborhood**), she still feels the need to be more "presentable" and to upkeep a beautiful, feminine, well-groomed appearance at formal meetings at work or school. Audrey's words indicate that lesbian mothers need to take into account the routine burden of proof under which they live as lesbian women – to pay attention to their external appearance to prove to the world that their sexual orientation is not a result of an inability to get a man:

Um... I do... I feel pressure if we go to a problematic meeting. With kindergarten teachers, for example, or at work.

It's really important to me that I look excellent. And I actually do come in with earrings and jewelry, all dolled up like that. Here, where we live, I can go out in pajamas, I don't care. Everyone knows that we're such good and smart mothers. But wherever there's a sense of representativeness, I do feel the need. I put more attention into how I dress. I come with makeup on, I go fix my hair. I feel like we have to be beautiful because of the stereotype that lesbians can't get a man or that they're ugly. I feel the need to be the opposite. And that's where I have run-ins with my feminism (laughs). It's theory, it's reality, and somehow in the middle I'm searching for my own way...

Nora, a member of the "third wave," stressed that even though it is hard for her to admit, she is still busy shaping the positive image she shows heterosexual society, because of a need to prove that mothers in same-sex families are just as good, if not better, than mothers in heterosexual ones. In other words, the work of lesbian mothers is still largely influenced by conformity to cultural meta-narratives that view fatherless families with two mothers as inferior, flawed, and lacking in family configuration. In which children inevitably grow up "miserable," which leaves them no choice but to function as impeccable citizens and outstanding mothers:

I think we.. that our image is um.. very important to us... being good citizens, having a good influence on the children, is very important to us, how our children end up is very important to us. It's like proving to the environment – look at how mentally healthy, how smart, sensitive, and developed a child of two mothers is! here, he has two mothers and it's just a bonus! not a loss! because people are very busy thinking: "What a miserable kid, he doesn't have a father." No, he's not miserable at all. Look how happy he is, how full of love he is and how much love he gets! like, I think like we... even if we won't admit it, we're busy trying to prove that we're good enough! as a couple of women, good enough and maybe even better than a man and woman raising children!

Nora specifically feels that she is always been evaluated and supervised by the social environment ("examining eye"), which expects her and her children to be "special" and to demonstrate exceptional qualities ("like caviar in a tuna market"), and which even rewards her with approval and reinforcement for demonstrating such behavior:

I like doing things from a place of what I want, and what's comfortable for me, but I do believe that there's some kind of examining eye that expects you to be something really special. People also keep telling us: "Wow, your child is really special!" or "So fun for your child – the mothers he has" and "What a special family!" and there's nothing we can do, they treat us like we're something special! something rare! like caviar in a tuna market, what can we do?!

Interestingly, Nora's "examining eye" is reminiscent of Jack's "Over-Eye" (Jack, 1991), which "pronounces harsh judgment on most aspects of a woman's authentic strivings" (ibid., p. 94). At the same time, we can hear Nora's implicit concern about how easy it is for the "examining eye" to turn the "specialness" of a family with two mothers from an asset and advantage into a limitation or obstacle.

Even a narrator who didn't want to think of herself as living under the "burden of proof ," admits to its existence when specifically asked about it. Sharon, a member of the second wave, admits that although she hadn't thought about it before, it could be that she unknowingly invests a lot in her children to show people that "the children are happy" and "normative," "even though they're growing up in a family with two mothers." She places special emphasis on her children's education and discipline in order to dispel cultural myths according to which every family needs a father to impose authority, boundaries, and discipline:

> *It's hard for me to say with certainty, maybe it's in my subconscious, that I have some need to show how okay things are and investing in the children, and "look, the children here are growing up okay and the children are normative and the children are happy and they're content and smiling, even though they're growing up in a family with two mothers." It could be that this is true. I never thought about it, but I wouldn't want my child to be the class clown and "well, look, he's growing up with two mothers, he doesn't have a father, he's lacking structure, he doesn't have any boundaries and that's why he's like that." I mean, it would really upset me to hear something like that. I think when you bring a child into this type of framework, even when you... it subconsciously exists. This need to show that everything's alright, and that the children will be happy and won't want for anything and that everything will be normal. Like, the kids need to be even more okay, to show everyone, "Guys, there are studies that show that this is okay" (laughs).*

Along with the "burden of proof" in heterosexual society, some narrators reported the burden of representation in the LGBTQ community. With the absence of models, some narrators felt pressure to be role models themselves, and sources of support and advice for young lesbian women and same-sex families at the start of their journeys. Tiffany, a member of the "first wave," said that for many years she and her partner felt that whenever they left the house, they should be a "role model" for lesbian families and consultants for lesbian women debating various issues, whether to have children, how to do it (co-parenting with a father or sperm donation), how to choose a sperm donor, requirements for adoption, etc. They ultimately grew tired of the burden and preferred to let other lesbian families continue their mission with the LGBTQ community:

For many years, I felt that we were some kind of symbol and example and that every time we go outside the house we should be a model for lesbian families. It's a type of burden. You're placed on some kind of pedestal, like a saint. It's not easy... it's definitely a major burden. I think that was one of the reasons we just stopped, we weren't in touch with the community anymore. After some... after we got back from a trip abroad. Sammy was 10 years old when we got back and we didn't want to do it anymore. We didn't have that need in ourselves anymore and it weighed down on us, that feeling of "wow" and "you guys have been together for so many years" and "what a big girl" and "what big kids, what a family." Like... it's heavy. For many years, we were a role model for women who wanted children and came to consult with us, and for women who had small children and we had older children, and for women who were debating about whether or not to get married and we were together for many years. And for women who were debating whether and how to have children – alone or in a relationship, with this kind of sperm or that kind of sperm, with that partner or this partner, or someone who wanted, couples

*who were considering guardianship and after that
couples who were considering adoption and after that...
like... and which name to take and how to change a name.
It's as though we went through every stage first. And if
not first, then second. So each of these steps always... like
we, we really, forged a path that was very pioneering but
like... so it always had to be presentable (smiling). At
some point, we just got tired. And there were, you know,
other couples, so we let them continue with it...*

The "burden of proof ," that is, the pressure described by the
narrators to be a shining example of normalcy and excellence, to
prove to the heterosexual society that they are worthy mothers,
as well as the burden of representation to the LGBTQ community, are not mentioned in Meyer's "minority stress" model, and
are rarely reported in the research and theoretical literature on
same-sex families. Thus, these findings expand Meyer's (1995,
2003) model of "minority stress" and add new dimensions
when it comes to planned same-sex families.

Trial and Error, Biological Inequity, and Internalized Homophobia in Relationships

In their public-representative self-portrait, the narrators tended
to highlight their androgynous personalities (a combination of
feminine and masculine traits) and the unique benefits of lesbian relationships and motherhood. However, careful attention to
their narratives, revealed that the lesbian family unit presented
them with unique challenges such as role confusion, trial and
error, role duplication, an excess of "feminine" energies and
functions (such as care, concern, understanding, containment),
which often came at the price of there being a lack of masculine energies and functions (such as assertiveness, practicality,

financial security), so that they were forced to redefine the division of burdens and roles in the family.

According to Olga, when the girls entered their lives, it shook up her relationship with her partner, and the fact that they were a pair of mothers quickly shifted from being an advantage to being a disadvantage. They each came with their own family model and a very clear concept of education and how to raise children, which led to "power wars" that, thanks only to effective couple's therapy, didn't end in separation:

> *At the relationship level, a child enters the picture, and it shakes up your whole world. When there are two, it's twice as much. So at first it seemed that we were actually a strong force because we were two women, and to a certain extent that was also true. Slowly, we got weaker. At some point the advantage became a disadvantage because we... each one of us had a clear vision of what to do with a child, each one was a lioness... It was clear to each of us how to raise children and when to spoil more and when to spoil less, when to give medicine, when not to give medicine... We came from two completely different homes. So each one had her own model. Even though it was clear to me that my parents are no model, but I came from there, so there are a lot of things that are hard to disconnect from. So there were many wars. We did couples' therapy at the time, we almost separated. But... we got through it. It wasn't easy but it's completely behind us.*

Sarah referred to the innovation and confusion involved in building a lesbian family unit, due to the lack of same-sex family models. According to her, the "masculine" functions such as, assertiveness, coldness, practicality, and economic security are not always fully or adequately represented:

I really think we're building something new. There's something archetypal about the man-woman family unit with its very structured roles, something very, um, something very established. Even the more modern families have very clear roles. And I feel like a lot of the time, I'm searching and trying things out with our family, because, you know, in a family with mothers, two mothers, the roles are unclear, they both do everything or nothing. For us, like, we both want to do everything for our daughter. Oh, and we both take on the maternal role, we're both very concerned about all sorts of things, like food, clothing, being giving to her, the whole thing about understanding and including her... There's a lot of that. But, you know, there are all sorts of male roles, that I believe are unclear to both of us. For example, let's say, when things get overheated at home (laughs), hysteria or tragedy – there's no one to come in and stop it, and for me, it's sometimes overkill. Or I don't know, something that will be, something more cold and practical. Gaia [her partner, A.P.], she's like more practical, but still, it's not practical enough, it's not enough... Let's just say, we take turns, each one of us takes on a different role each time. But, sometimes, I have a desire for there to be more clarity here... And like when it comes to financials, for instance, sometimes, I want someone to support me (laughs)... Like, I want some guy to provide for me... But it's a fantasy, because even in reality, men don't always provide...

Meanwhile, Ramona examined the complexity of a same-sex lesbian relationship through several prisms:

The first few years were not easy, they really were years when we had to figure out how, how it would look, and there were always so many questions and always so much... and nothing could be taken for granted. And in general, I believe that it's not so simple with women. I mean, you always bring with you your relationship with your mother... We're very much in a process of trying to build something different, but it's hard because once you become a parent you suddenly become a bit like your own parents... um... so in terms of roles, that's basically how it was, until two or three years ago. There's that film: "Black Swan." Have you seen that movie? they show all the... you know, the replication, the replication that there is between mother and daughter but also... it's kind of like, you know, seeing a lot of things in the mirror. You see your mother, you suddenly see your woman, and you... you know, you do something, and someone else does the same thing, but it's not the same thing, because it's not the same person. Now there's also the thing with the kids. There are many, you know, everyone deals with the kids differently. When you're totally different, you deal with kids differently, too. So I'm the type of person who lets things slide, and Varda, my partner, is very strict and everything with her has a limit. And then it became, you know, we started fighting about the parenting aspect as well. Because for Varda, having agreements was very important, and for me, you know, emotion was more important, and it became difficult. So it's true that maybe, you know, it's something that a lot of couples go through after many years of being together, and okay, there's a need here for working on communication, but I think being of the same gender also comes into play here...

Evidence of trial and error and role confusion among mothers in same-sex families in Israel can also be found in Livni's research

(2004). According to Livni, in the absence of a clear family model, it is up to every pair of mothers in planned lesbian families to pave their own path, and invent their own desired way of developing their family structure. Paving a new family path raises tension and conflicts between the partners, and requires a re-evaluation of family roles and structures, which are often taken for granted by couples in heterosexual families.

Biological inequality posed another challenge to lesbian relationships. Although the narrators interpret their identities as co-mothers for all intents and purposes in their public-representative self-portrait, dismissing the biology's meaning or influence, multiple readings of the narratives, showed that the biological component shaped their relationships with spouses and children quite significantly, whether consciously and voluntarily or unconsciously and involuntarily.

In families with one biological mother and one non-biological mother, the non-biological mother was generally busy building her relationship with the children, establishing her position as a co-mother and finding her place, not just among the families of origin and social environment, but first and foremost vis-à-vis her spouse/the biological mother and the children. Jane (a non-biological mother of a 6-year-old boy in her early 30s) used building and gardening metaphors, such as "grow," "carve," "find my place," "maintained," to describe the effort she put into building a relationship with her (non-biological) son, and finding her place in the family:

> *My relationship with Ian has grown over the years. Since I'm not his biological mother and... Daria spends much more time with him. Both today and during the early years. She was at home with him for two years and they had, they still have a very, very strong bond. So I had to carve out some place there. We basically had to find my*

place in this relationship, together. That's why I say that the relationship grew... From the first moment it was clear that I was his mother and I was a parent, and I took care of him, and I cared for him, and I did things for him. But because I'm with him less, the relationship had to be maintained.

Adriana described her bond with her (non-biological) children as strong but "different" from her partner's:

I have a very strong bond with the children, especially now. I've been spending a lot of time with them for two years now, but... I think it's still a different relationship. We wanted one so bad, especially with the firstborn, Ollie. We thought a lot about what a "biological mother" is and what a "non-biological mother" is, and what to do, what to watch out for, and what not to do, and how I would feel if... We weren't afraid of those things at all. Hellen [spouse, A.P.] was afraid of the brass tacks, the caregiving, of how and what to do, to breastfeed and care, and all that. And I'm not at all, because I take care of children from a very young age, and I wasn't afraid of the practical side. I was afraid of... it was because I took care of so many children for very long periods of time in a very intensive way, that I was afraid of just not loving them... Like, what in this process would actually make me love them? I will know how to take care of them, but what, what will happen that will make me love them? That was my fear before Ollie was born. But when he was born, that didn't happen at all... Something I didn't have, for example, starting breastfeeding and all that, we talked a lot about it. We even thought maybe, you know, that I would try to breastfeed since we'd heard all kinds of stories. Um...

*And in the end we decided not to do it. But it was very
important for me to have a bottle, for example. So I could
also be a part of it all. But these are things where we have
enough openness between us, so we can say what bothers
us and argue about it and then find a solution that works
for us both...*

When Ella (a non-biological mother of a 7-year-old boy, a
5-year-old boy, and a 1-year old girl in her late 40s) was asked
about her fears about the future, she said she feared that her
children would one day offend her, saying that she is "not even
[their] mother":

*I have a certain fear that they'll suddenly realize at some
point that biology bears some meaning. I have a fear, just
a phobia, that they'll suddenly say: "You're not even our
mother." It scares me. But um... I'm immune to it because
I know so well that I'm their mother. And they know it too.
So I guess if they ever used something like that against me,
it would just be, you know, something that hurts in the
moment. And they may very much regret it and feel sorry
a minute later, or even two days later, it doesn't matter, or
even two months or even two years... I'm aware that it can
happen and happens because kids are constantly like that,
like, they can switch parents, like who they prioritize, it's
also kind of a game of control for them as well. I would be
a little sad about it, it scares me a little, but we'll deal with
it. I guess it will happen at some point...*

While the non-biological mother was busy building her relationship with the children, establishing herself as a co-mother,
and finding her place with the biological mother and children,
the biological mother faced a challenge of her own: Understand

135

what it means to be a mother in a family with more than one mother, and to redefine her motherhood work. For Nellie, "being a mother in a pair" (a mother who is not one) is a unique and complex experience:

> *The experience of being mothers together is a strange experience. I haven't spoken about it but it's like... wait, "there's only one mom," isn't there? what does it say about me as a mother that there isn't just one at home? and I really feel like my motherhood is different because we're two. Because there's another alternative, because I'm not just one. Because in our culture, the concept of "there's only one mom" is so inherent in the role of mother, and then suddenly "being a mother in a pair" is a completely different role.*

Hellen (a biological mother of a 9-year-old boy, a 5-year-old girl, and a 1-year-old boy in her late 30s) referred to the fact that her place as a biological mother, alongside a non-biological mother, has also undergone development and changes, and is something needs to be constantly considered and built and defined anew, is she "another mother?" when is she the authority and when is she not? etc.:

> *I think that sometime, let's say in the last year or two, I began having funny questions a bit in delay. In the beginning, when our first son was born, it was really important for me to establish Adriana's [spouse, A.P.] place as a mother, because I gave birth to him and it was very not self-explanatory. And the energies were always directed there. And somewhere in the last few years I said, hmm my place as a biological mother next to a non-biological mother is something that needs to be*

*thought about and built and defined and that these are
things that are relatively new. Especially now that I'm
more of the "dad" because I'm actually less at home and
the main breadwinner and like, the balance between us,
which at first was very precise, has kind of changed. And
it's challenging. In the years when the children were very
young, my place as a mother was very clear to me. I mean,
I gave birth, I breastfed, um... the bond was very, very self-
explanatory. They grew up, and as they get older, there is
some distance that forms that is healthy but distancing.
And me, as I tend to say, Adriana and I used to be very
much the same – in how we took care of them, in when
we were present at home. It's changed a lot. They are now
in frameworks much less often because they're bigger, and
I work more hours outside the home and spend relatively
few hours with them. So the relationship has changed
a lot. Now I'm a less central figure in their day-to-day
lives. Now, how am I a mother in all this? especially when
there's a mother, it's not like there isn't. I'm a mom that's
not around a lot." I'm "another mom." When am I an
authority figure? when am I not? in general, how do I fit
into the flow here at home, which often takes place without
me, and then suddenly I come around, and well, there are
all kinds of customs that I'm not a part of?*

In families where the narrator is simultaneously a biological mother and a non-biological mother, there would often be a tendency to make a distinction between "my children" and "her children." This distinction is expressed in different attachment styles with the biological children compared to that with the non-biological ones. While the attachment process with the biological children is shaped in a direct and unmediated way through the physical connection (pregnancy, childbirth, breastfeeding, tending to physical needs), the attachment process with the non-biological children had to be paved and constructed through thought, desire, and intention of all parties involved. The genetic similarity in appearance, personality traits, preferences, and behavior would also often form a closeness and strong emotional bond between the biological mother and her biological children, and pose a difficult challenge for the non-biological mother, not to mention the differences in expectations, attitudes, and reactions of the families of origin and social environment to the biological mother, compared to that to the non-biological one. Without being fully accepted as a co-mother with equal rights, and without intensive support and assistance from the biological mother (and children), there have been cases where the non-biological mother reported feeling distant, "not belonging," and discriminated against, a situation that often led to serious crises in the relationship and family.

According to Nina (a non-biological mother of a 5-year-old girl and a biological mother of a 1-year-old girl, in her early 30s), biology and physiology definitely shape biological motherhood as a different experience from non-biological motherhood. From the beginning, her spouse/the biological mother formed a symbiotic relationship with the eldest daughter, Annie, who pushed Nina (the non-biological mother) aside, giving her the status of "second best mom" and made her constantly struggle for her place. Her partner's use of the "biological card" and the distinction she makes between "my girl" and "your girl" causes Nina great anguish and frustration, and provoke much tension and conflicts between the partners. Echoes of that anguish can be found in the fact that Nina burst into tears several times during the interview and found it difficult to calm down:

It's different, it's different being a biological mother and a non-biological mother because on a physiological level and on a ... Look, when I walk around with Doreen it's clear that I gave birth to her. With Annie, we're not very similar. But I always say, "This is my daughter," I don't say, "This is the daughter my partner gave birth to" (crying). So yes, there is a difference in the physiological sense but it's not that I love Doreen more than Annie, it's a different love. My mother would say that too, it's not like there's a favorite child, she has different relationships, we're three siblings, she has a different relationship with each one of us. Mary [partner, A.P.] formed a kind of symbiotic relationship with Annie. We're very, very close, she loves me and looks for me and all that, but the symbiotic bond does create some kind of division. It's really annoying (crying), so annoying, I'm really not a complainer, but I've become one. And the best example, she doesn't do it as much today, but the best example is that if Annie cries, for example, and I hold her, she'll take her. And I don't do that with Doreen. I think about what's good for Doreen, it's better for her if it's not like that, she doesn't need only me to comfort her. I'm also confident in where I stand, so I don't need to. Look, I can tell you that most of our arguments are about education. I run a very 'tough love' framework, and with boundaries and manners, because it builds values. She can tell Annie "no" and a second later, "Okay, so take something else." And I go out of my mind, smoke comes out of my ears. Then she has tantrums and when I explain to her where the tantrums come from, "No, no, no, that's her personality." And when it comes to education, it's very hard for me that I'm like second best. For anything I say, either Mary will say the opposite or she will ask me, "No, why so? let's do it differently." One example is that she kind of has the last say with Annie because, like, she's the... but as for Doreen, it's just amazing, because, for example, with Doreen, she suddenly started asking me a lot of things, "So, I'll give her a bath? should I make her a bottle?" I say to her, "Why are you asking me? I mean, with Annie you never asked. If you felt she wanted a bottle, then you made her one." "No, I want to hear." Meaning, I think she's acting the way she'd like me to act. And I act the way I think people are supposed to. She claims that even if both of us were the biological mothers, she would do this, but I'm not sure... It's very complex. I guess even for straight people, when they have hardships and they don't want to break up the family because of the children, and also with them there's one parent who is more strict and one parent who is more lenient with the children, it's clear to me that it's the same thing. But there's always the biological card... It always comes up, both in terms of families and society.

Talia (a non-biological mother of an 8-year-old boy and a 2.5-year-old boy, and a biological mother of a 4-year-old boy, in her early 30s) said it took her a while to feel like a "full mom" to Shawn, her youngest non-biological child, until he accepted her:

With Tom the eldest, I don't feel that there is any difference between me and Norma Lee [her spouse, A.P.] in terms of motherhood. Tom wasn't breastfed by Norma Lee or me. We both bottle-fed him. Um... with Ron it was... since I breastfed him, it was different. He was right beside me and I didn't let him go so much. I felt like I needed to be with him while he was breastfeeding and he breastfed almost all the time. It was like... there was a bit of conflict there but then it worked out... that's it. So after Ron and after

Tom, came Shawn, and that's when I felt it big time. Big time. Norma Lee breastfed him and I felt, "Wow, what a difference." What a difference it is to be Tom's mom, to be Ron's mom, and then to be Shawn's mom. Shawn was glued to Norma Lee and I felt that I had no part there and I really... And then I was able to understand what she had told me about Ron. Although with Ron I will emphasize that at the age of three and a half months I went back to work and left him with her all week, so somewhere along the lines, at a much quicker point, she regained an equal share in motherhood. But it makes a difference. And with Shawn, it was... it was terrible for me...just awful, terrible, difficult. He was glued to Norma Lee and nothing I, I couldn't put him to sleep, I couldn't... I don't remember about changing him or that, but he almost didn't want anything from me, he just wanted Norma Lee. It was terribly frustrating. Until it got to the point that... that he accepted me, but it was much later. It was much later that he let me in as a full mom or gave me a feeling, or I gave myself, I don't know who it depends on here, but that I could also feel the ... this parenting thing with him in an amazing way.

Toby shared that when she gets angry, she wakes up with "little voices shouting in the back of the head," saying what the environment says: "yours" and "hers." These "voices" make her hypersensitive and react more strongly to unwanted behavior of the non-biological daughter, compared to the biological daughter:

When the older one does something I don't like, or teases, even at her age, however small she is, there is a little Toby in me that sometimes gets hurt, that sometimes, again, gets angry. It doesn't have to be this way, I know... I'm a big girl, I'm a big woman, it's not... and just as it comes, that's how it goes. Because my little one, that is, the one I gave birth to, my biological one, they're sisters, half biological sisters, and they grow up together as sisters in every respect. So it can suddenly come, but then it blurs... even if there are small voices shouting in the back of the head, saying all kinds of things... What the environment says, when you belong, there are those who say: "yours" and "hers." So if there are, sometimes, you know, passing thoughts about "hers," "mine," or something like that, it's bad and hurtful and unpleasant, and you go back to being the "little me." In such cases, it comes out... but, for the most part, it doesn't happen, definitely not.

Confirmation of biological inequality causing significant stress in the lives of mothers in planned lesbian families, can be found in the study of Pelka (2009). Pelka analyzed partners/co-motherhood relationships in planned lesbian families in the United States by comparing three types of lesbian families: Couples who adopted children, couples who had children through artificial insemination, and couples who had children through in vitro fertilization (one mother donated an egg and the other her uterus). The results of her research show that lesbian couples who had children in a family constellation with biological asymmetry, that is, a biological mother and non-biological mother (artificial insemination), reported a higher degree of jealousy and power struggles than lesbian couples who had children in a family constellation with biological symmetry, meaning that both mothers are biological mothers (in vitro fertilization), or where neither mother is a biological mother (adoption).

Livni (2004) studied mothers in planned lesbian families in Israel, who had children through artificial insemination (one biological mother and one non-biological). According to her, the excessive importance attributed to the biological connection in Israeli society tends to create asymmetrical power struggles between the biological mother and the non-biological one, and raise tension and conflicts among the spouses on education and childcare, relationships with families of origin, speaking in public ("outward speech"), etc. Her research findings highlight the power the biological mother has in granting or denying the legitimacy of the co-mother.

Finally, careful listening to the narratives of the narrators showed that some of them internalized negative social attitudes on same-sex orientation. Internalized homophobia is expressed, among others, in how they haven't made peace with their same-sex orientation and different marital and family constellations. That lack of acceptance was often an added source of mental, stress, which affected the marital relationship and the division of roles in the home.

Difficulties in self-acceptance of same-sex orientation and different family constellations can be gleaned from Nina's words. Nina described her partner as someone who all her life defined herself as "straight in every one of her bones" and who endured a deep mental crisis, as a result of a sudden infatuation she had with a woman in her midlife. According to Nina, her partner does not define herself as a lesbian woman to this day, and has difficulty accepting the "lesbian family experience." The clash between Nina's self-acceptance and her partner's lack of peace and self-acceptance, affects every aspect of their marital and family life and creates a lot of tension between them:

Look, my story is very simple because I've been a lesbian from day 1, real textbook stuff, tomboy, into basketball, only likes boys' clothes and boys' toys, and blah blah blah. For Mary, the story is complex and long. She discovered herself midlife, and she didn't exactly discover herself, because she fell in love with someone, another woman, not me, and that's a good thing, she fell in love with someone and suddenly it flipped everything on its head. And she had a boyfriend for three years, they almost got married. She's someone who was straight in every one of her bones who suddenly went through an internal, mental crisis, I don't know what. So for her, I mean, everything is much more complicated. She doesn't define herself as a lesbian at all. The whole lesbian family experience is very difficult for her, meaning, it's not something that is obvious to her. To me it's obvious. It's very clear to me that this is a family and two mothers and two children, and for her it's less... I think that if she was 100% lesbian then most of the things that were hard for her to deal with, wouldn't exist at all, like the whole issue of family roles, who gives birth and who's the breadwinner, and who is the main caretaker and all that sort of things. Obviously every relationship experiences burnout and there're hardships and there are this, so when someone is not 100% accepting of themselves, it's even harder...

Concern about the effects of sexual orientation and fatherlessness and the pressure to raise 'straight' children

In the dominant narratives of the public-representative self-portrait, the narrators presented their choice to create a fatherless lesbian family as the most natural, obvious, and desirable choice for them. However, listening to "marginal," partial or silenced narratives, revealed that some narrators faced doubts and hesitations about what the appropriate family configuration is for them, and devoted considerable time and resources to researching the topic. This investigation included browsing relevant websites, reading studies and professional literature, talking to community members before and after parenthood, consulting with a child psychologist, etc. In fact, nearly half of the population in the current study (18 narrators, representing 45%) explored the option of forming a same-sex family with an active father figure, or known sperm donor: 10 narrators considered incorporating a present and active father figure into the same-sex family constellation, and eight additional narrators examined the possibility of using a known sperm donor from abroad.

The hesitations and intensive investigation of some of the narrators illuminated their "natural choice" of building a fatherless lesbian family in a different light. A default position that is largely dictated by external institutions such as the State and the judicial system. The legal system in Israel does not allow two mothers to adopt each other's biological children, under conditions in which the child has a biological father. The State of Israel does not offer programs for a known sperm donor, who can be contacted at the age of 18. Using a sperm donor from a known sperm donor from abroad, incurs a higher financial cost and is not an option for anyone who cares about the sperm donor being Jewish and/or Israeli. In other cases, other considerations (difficulty in finding a suitable candidate for a father figure, disagreements between spouses, etc.) that dictated the choice of the current family constellation.

These findings are consistent with claims by researchers such as Esterberg (2008), according to which the ability of lesbian families to build diverse and flexible family structures, is largely limited by the legal system, which offers a limited window of opportunity for lesbian couples to establish legal parental relationships with their children. Based on these findings, it would not be unreasonable to assume that if the legal reality in Israel were more flexible and recognizes family configurations consisting of three (or more) parents of a child, and if more diverse sperm donation programs existed in Israel, such as a non-anon-ymous sperm donation, some (but not all) of the narrators would choose to build a family with a father present or with the help of a known donor.

Some narrators reported mixed feelings, doubts, or concerns about the impact of fatherlessness. There were narrators who expressed concern that their children would accuse them of wrongdoings, because they had "deprived" them of a father fig-ure. This concern led some narrators to increase involvement of male family figures (a grandfather, uncle, etc.) in their lives, and even to look for male mentors outside the family (a teach-er, coach, counselor, or young mentor). Zara, for example, not-ed that there were times when she was tormented by guilt and thoughts that she might have rushed in choosing her current family configuration. Over time, she taught herself to relax, to accept reality as it is, and to trust her own strength, that of her spouse and her daughters to cope with the difficulties:

> Me, I had... I've had periods where I feel like I've done the girls an injustice, that maybe it's not good, maybe I rushed, maybe ... everything I experienced has brought me to this point and they're just a product paying the price and... and they didn't, and it's like I harmed them. Things like that. But... I learned to like come, to bring myself to this place of like, okay, this is what it is now. It's true. It's true that it would be nicer if I was straight and met a man and I could bring them an ideal and perfect family of mom and dad and... and everything would have worked out. Yes, yes. It would've been easier. That's for sure. It's an easier life. This life. But this is the situation and I cannot change it. So now we have to make the best of this situation. I'm not going to freak out about it, "Oh no, what have I done?" and now go look for some kind of

*framework, you know, of... no, they will cope and we will
cope together, with everything there is.*

Lily brought up the doubts and fears she had about the consequences of raising a child in a fatherless family when facing
other people's reactions. Her partner helped her dispel at least
some of her fears by reinforcing the aspect of motherly love:

> *When I met Ella and she told me she wanted to be a
> mother, it made me a little worried at first, I said, "What,
> won't the child be miserable?" ... All the stigmatic thoughts
> we immediately say, "A child without a father!" "How
> will everyone react??" and all these things... I remember
> we were discussing this in an online chat and Ella wrote
> me a sentence that got engraved in me: "Isn't motherly
> love the best thing in the world? so imagine that times
> 2!" and that's it, for me that was the thing that... like
> this sentence... so, okay, the issue of children is closed as
> far as I'm concerned. That pretty much dissolves all my
> hesitations on the matter.*

At a later stage, they explored the option of raising a child in a
constellation that involved a biological father, but rejected it for
practical reasons when they realized that the spouse would not
be able to adopt the children and receive legal and social recognition as another mother:

> *At a much later stage, when we really started talking brass
> tacks after a few years, we tried examining the options
> available to us as a lesbian couple: The sperm bank versus a
> known donor who would be active or inactive in the child's
> life. And we decided that it would be better for us not to
> have a father figure present at all in order to reinforce both*

of our roles in parenting and to create equality between the two of us. We knew we wouldn't have the legal option to adopt in a situation like that. It was clear to us that if you opt for a constellation that includes a biological father, then the non-biological mother automatically gets "demoted." In other words, she won't be considered a mother in any respect, nothing would help... and that's not the model we aspired to have for our family.

Today, her eldest son's exaggerated interest in male figures and his explicit statements that he would rather grow up in a family with a father than a family with two mothers, arouse sadness and pity in Lily for him. She hopes that he will find comfort in having another brother and not being the only son in the family:

I can tell you that Daniel [eldest son, A.P.] really relates to male figures. I think on some level, Daniel is, yes, he's missing... He'd be happy if he had a father (said feebly)... he also says this, he says: "I didn't want two moms, I'd rather have a dad." It could be that somewhere, maybe he's a bit of a poor kid because of it. Well, maybe "poor" is too big a word, but he might lack some... it's a little sad for me to hear, I can't tell you it isn't... Why does it make me sad too? because I have a really strong bond with my father. I was very much a daddy's girl and understand his desire for masculine energy, I can relate to that. But there's not much I can do about that. This is the family we chose to build! this is the family I can give my son! I can't just make a father appear from nowhere, and he'll have to live with that. There's nothing you can do about it. Everyone has to deal with shortcomings and things that they want but can't have... By the way, on a related note, we really hoped our second child would also be a boy. We really wanted that so he wouldn't be the only boy in the family. So when they told us it was a boy, we were so happy!

Ramona also had to give up raising her children in a family with a father for practical reasons. The man she proposed it to refused, and she couldn't find suitable alternative candidates who could serve as a father figure to her children:

By us, the children don't have a father and they don't have... it was a so-called anonymous donation. It wasn't easy to actually decide whether we'd have a known donor or not, whether there would be a father in this story or not. I mean, we argued quite a bit about it, as usual... (laughs), but we decided not to do it with a known donor. Even in retrospect, we saw in the end that there was no man around who we were really in touch with and was actually a good fit to be a potential father for our children (smiles). That's what ultimately convinced me. Of course there's this fantasy about the children having a father. But when I look around, I'm like, okay, I have a great partner who I'm very devoted to, how many men are there around me who I'd actually like to have a kid with? There was one, and I might have brought up the idea a bit, and it really didn't pan out, and I think to this day he has no children. He really wasn't on that track. So... you know, the fantasy was there but we made the decision to bring a girl or boy to the world without a father, it's really a major decision.

Ramona believes that although her children might have a "gap" in their identity, the love, protection, warmth, and values they have instilled in them, will compensate for it, and will have a more significant impact on their lives:

> *It's something I believe will accompany them for the rest of their lives, um... this "gap" they have in their identity or this lack of information regarding the biological baggage they carry. So there are all kinds of things you think. Like, wow, it's still not easy bringing a child into the world like this with such givens, which will definitely have a lifelong impact. But you want to believe that really, you know, the great love that you give them and the protection, the home, you know, this warmth and the values, that it's something that will accompany them and give them strength. They'll be the ones to decide what kind of family they want to build for themselves. Assuming that generally about 10% of life's circumstances contribute to or detract from our happiness, then fine (smiles). If it's only 10%, then that's fine.*

The children's adolescence was mentioned as a particularly threatening time of the children making potential accusations regarding paternal absence or family differences. Norma Lee expressed great fear about her sons growing up and complaining that she is raising them in a family constellation without a man/father. The fear of these accusations and the desire to expose their sons to male figures they can identify with, has led her and her partner to seek out a mentor for their older son to do "men's things" with him:

> *I don't know if I should mention it, but there really is the issue of – what will happen when the children ask... um... in the future, who donated the sperm, this is a very big fear... As far as I'm concerned, how do I cope with a child, a boy, in adolescence who will come from this place of... that he'll, like, complain "Why is it like this?!" and "I don't have a father." I can tell you that we are trying these days*

to find a male figure for the older son. A young man who
can be there whom he can identify with, go out with and
do masculine things, men's things. To provide some kind
of solution.

Whether these shortcomings are real or imagined, some narrators have internalized cultural myths about needing a father for
their children to have proper psychological and sexual development (especially boys) and try to compensate for that with various substitutes. Naturally, the very fact that the mother feels as
though the child is living with a "lack" or a "gap in their identity"
can permeate to the child and become a self-fulfilling prophecy.

In fact, a significant number of narrators were particularly preoccupied and concerned with their children's sexual and
gender identities. They emphasized that even though they give
their children the freedom to choose their own games and activities, regardless of gender norms, and even though they would
have no problem accepting a child who is gay or lesbian, they
see no indication that their children bear same-sex sexual orientations. Even the few narrators who participated in radical
feminist and anti-sexist education, tended to highlight their
children's heterosexual identity.

Rose (a non-biological mother of a 16-year-old girl and biological mother of a 12-year-old girl, in her late 40s) said she was
troubled by the question of how her sexual orientation and their
constellation of a fatherless family affect her daughters' psychological identification processes and the development of their future sexual identities and relationships. She said she wouldn't
want her two daughters to be lesbians. If the two girls "decide"
to be lesbians, she will suspect that she hadn't exposed them
enough to men. But at the end of her remarks, she is careful to
point out that she does not see any indications of her daughters
having tendencies towards same-sex sexual orientations:

I'd like to know about identity. Like who do they identify with and to what extent? and how much is the lesbian thing affecting their identity? I'm pretty sure that if they both decide to be lesbians, then I'll think that they perhaps didn't have enough contact with men, not enough of that type of attachment, and that would make me a bit upset. I'd like for them to experience, say, relationships with men as well, that's something I would like them to experience. Like... there's this thing where you try to figure it out at a young age, so... (goes silent). I think that... I wouldn't want both of them to be lesbians. I'll suspect that it's something that... even though statistically it's like the same probability, but I'd find it a shame that... maybe they didn't meet enough men, didn't feel enough of an attachment to men, and didn't develop that option. But, to me neither of them seem lesbian... certainly not Leah, and not Nala either...

Lily reported that from the beginning, it was very important to her and her partner not to give in to gender norms, and to give their children the freedom of choice to experiment with various games and accessories. However, in the same breath, she adds that their older son is very "masculine," while the other son is more sensitive and likes to wear the mothers' shoes, but does not "go too far" as to put kerchiefs on his head, like their friends' son, who they have no doubt is homosexual (but their son is not):

First of all, this is something we talked about even before we had children, it's very important for me to give the children the opportunity to choose and not... We really don't go by gender norms. But it's funny, because I got... especially Daniel, the oldest son, I got a son who's very...

152

into cars, woah, wars. In other words, there was no room for doubt at all... Let's say Owen, the other son, who is more sensitive like that, he wants to start walking around in our shoes and stuff like that. I mean, I'll never limit him in his playtime, I mean... he doesn't go too far and, like, ask to wear kerchiefs on his head or something... Like, we were just by our friends, where we said, "The son must be gay!" because his game is to set the table and then put kerchiefs on his head, and when his father finds out about this, he'll flip out...

Even a narrator like Daria, who educates her son to resist gender stereotypes and encourages him to experiment with behaviors stereotypically associated with the opposite gender (pink clothes, applying nail polish, etc.) in public (in the street, at kindergarten), came to the conclusion that there is no way that he could be gay because "he loves girls":

I won't let people tell my son what's right for a boy and what's right for a girl. He wears pink and loves it and I teach him to respond. He began responding, too. He already has the confidence. Even in kindergarten, kids tell him that pink is for girls, and he explicitly tells them: "It's not for girls. All the colors are for everyone. I'll keep wearing pink." He also said... out of spite ... he said this yesterday (smiling), that he "did it on purpose" and he put on nail polish. On every finger. He told me, "Mom, I want to put it on my toes, too." And I'm happy. This is something that I passed on to him, and I will pass on to all our children. And I don't care; he can wear makeup, too, for all I care. But there's no way he'll be gay, he won't be gay. He's crazy about girls.

The narrators' reassurances about their children's normative sexual identity ("there's no way he'll be gay") could be considered a "defense mechanism" against cultural accusations of possibly harming their children's sexual and gender development.[50] The tendency of mothers and fathers in same-sex families to prove that their children are healthy and "normal" (i.e., heterosexual and cisgender)[51] and to dispel concerns about the negative effects growing up in same-sex families has on children's psychosexual development, has been studied and described in same-sex families in Europe.[52]

It seems there is a considerable amount of internalized homophobia related to the burden of proof aspect. Lesbian mothers seem to have accepted the notion that there is shame in same-sex orientation and have made every effort to declare themselves clear of this offense. In the process, they often fell prey themselves to gender and sexual stereotypes, such as Lily's assumption that wearing kerchiefs indicates homosexuality in a boy.

Adriana was one of the few narrators who dared speak about her son's non-normative gender behavior, and her and her partner's constant conflict regarding it. Adriana's words imply that the cruelty of calculating one's "burden of proof" is obvious. As lesbians, Adriana and her partner would like to allow their son to freely explore his sexuality and behave according to his preferences. Yet, Adriana knows full well that evidence of her child's non-normative sexual or gender identity can be used against her as proof of flawed or defective parenting:

---

50. Schnitzer, 1998; Wells, 2001.

51. Cisgender is a term used to describe people who feel that their gender identity corresponds with their biological sex, as opposed to transgender.

52. Clarke, 2002; Clarke and Kitzinger, 2004.

*The oldest son has always... stood out in many respects.
Now he also has a... we'll call it a feminine side, I don't
know. But like at a certain age, his favorite color was pink.
Now that's very, very unusual for a 4-year-old boy, okay?
it's not (laughs). He insisted on it. Like, he wanted pink
sandals, okay? even if the salesman told him okay, they're
his size but he's a boy and he has boy sandals for him.
No, this is the color that he likes. And we have questions
about this... Like, on the one hand, it's very unpleasant
for a family like ours to restrict him. That would be most
absurd. Are we going to tell him that that's not okay? on
the other hand, how much can this harm him? and we
had Purim [a Jewish holiday where it's customary to dress
up in costume, A.P.] last year... um... he always invested
so much in all his costumes and he drives us crazy for 6
months about what he wants to wear, and he goes and
plans it and paints it. And then he decided he would dress
up as a girl. And here's another question. What do we do
with that? I mean, on the one hand, we say – that would
be absolutely crazy if we tell him "no." On the other hand,
what will people say about him? What will people say
about us?*

Compared to the issue of same-sex orientation, regarding which
narrators said they would have no problem accepting a boy who
is gay or a girl who is lesbian (i.e., same as them), some narrators said that they would have an issue accepting a child who
is transgender (i.e., different from them). According to Dori, if
her daughter, Natalie, identifies as transgender, she will need to
do some "inner work" to accept her. Dori emphasizes that the
transgender experience is dissimilar to the lesbian experience,
that it is an entirely different experience:

If Natalie grows up and tells me at age 17: "Mom, I think I'm a lesbian," that's fine. Did you see the movie about transgenders? I'm really into it. Have you seen it? kids, not kids, but all types of people – transgenders – who literally transformed their gender. They showed the surgery of a girl who wanted to be a "he," and became a "he" in the end. It's... it's really like... let them be lesbian or gay, let them be whatever they want, to live well. When it comes to transgenders – I still need to work on myself! It's – I need to work on myself. It's – I have to see how, how it's experienced. But also, I don't think I'd have a problem, I mean... by the time she grows up, I'll already know how to work with it. But that's something that – wow! it's stuff that... It's not our experience, as lesbians – we don't experience that – it's, wow, it's something completely different!

Similarly, Sherry clarified that even though she would have no problem accepting a child who is homosexual or a girl who is lesbian, it would be very difficult for her to support a child who is transgender. Sherry has difficulty accepting people who do not wholly identify with one of the genders. To her, it seems as though people like that are stuck "in the middle" of some kind of "twilight zone." With these remarks, Sherry demonstrates acceptance of heteronormative standards of sexuality and gender, according to which a person can belong to one of two rigid binary gender categories, a "man" or a "woman":

Look, if Noah comes along one day and says, "I'm gay," I'll have no problem with that... or if Natasha tells me she's a lesbian... I only want them to live happy lives, let them be happy. I would have a problem with a transgender child, that would be hard for me. You know, it's very strange, exactly two or three weeks ago, I don't know, we were driving down a street, not Ha-Etzel Street, on Haganah Road I think, and a transgender person was crossing the road with high-heels, tight pants, a shirt like this tied here with a bow, and hair that was like brushed back, you can immediately tell. And then, like, the thought came to me and we were in the car and I said to Sharon [her spouse, A.P.] like, this is something I can't seem to comprehend. Like, it's much easier for me to understand someone who decides to, for example, have a sex change, like going all the way with it, and I told her, not that I know or have gotten to know anyone like this, but I don't understand that, like, being in the "middle." Like, from their point of view, I have no doubt that they have a very strong feminine orientation, so like why not take it all the way, how you feel and what you want? I mean, a lot of people look to me, from the outside, right? like that they're stuck in some kind of "twilight zone." But, I am not familiar with this world, I can't tell you anything about it...

Both Dori and Sherry expressed reservations about transgender people and distinguished themselves from them. It can be argued that the contrast between them and the transgender community helps them stretch and expand the space of "norm" to include lesbians and homosexuals, while at the same time drawing a new boundary between them and transgender people, placing the latter in the space of "pathology." Such a strategy involves a deep internalization of heterosexism and transphobia.

The concept that queer children do not necessarily find support from lesbian mothers is confirmed in various studies. Kuva-lanka and Goldberg (2009) studied the experiences of LGBTQ+ youth with LGBTQ+ parents in the United States. Some of the participants reported that they did not perceive or use their parents as sources of assistance when it came to building their non-normative sexual/gender identity.

The experience of increased stress among children and challenges of discourse with them

Multiple readings of the narratives, using "On the Listening Guide: A voice-centered relational method,[53] showed that while the children enjoyed the many benefits of lesbian relationships and families, they also shared many of the hardships, stress, and challenges with their mothers, to varying degrees and intensities. In fact, it can be determined that if mothers in same-sex families face personal stigma, their children face associative stigma. Associative stigma (Goffman, 1963), also known in the research literature as 'courtesy stigma' or 'affiliate stigma,' is a negative social label a person carries due to a close relationship they have with another person with a stigma. Associative stigma, though to a lesser extent than personal stigma, can be a source of psychological distress (Quinn and Chaudoir, 2009). Various studies have shown that parents of children with disabilities; spouses, siblings, and children of mentally ill people; as well as caregivers of people with AIDS, have reported suffering from stigma, including feelings of shame, the need to keep their identity hidden, and the belief that others are evading or are likely to avoid them due to their "associative stigma" (ibid, 2009). In the same vein, I argue that children in fatherless same-sex families face what I call "affiliated minority stress": that is, they are exposed, directly or indirectly, to many of the elements of "minority stress" to which mothers are exposed, albeit generally less intensely and frequently.

---

53. Gilligan and Eddy, 2017; Gilligan, et al., 2003.

For the most part, the children did not express their difficulties or stressors with open, explicit statements. They could be gleaned from implicit statements, recurring questions, and maladaptive behaviors, such as crying, aggressive conduct, concealing family differences, and seclusion. The children's coping patterns were greatly influenced by variables such as the child's gender (boys vs. girls), the child's age (early childhood, elementary school, adolescence), their position in the family (firstborns vs. younger children), personality traits (extrovert vs. introvert), and family coping patterns (active vs. inactive families in the public sphere). Generally, the firstborns had to deal with stigmas and bearing the "burden of proof" of normalcy and excellence, to a greater extent than their younger siblings. In quite a few cases, they are the ones who paved the way towards social acceptance for their siblings.

Rose described the different emotional struggles each of her daughters deals with. The youngest, who is already quite "different" in her character and behavior (a basketball player, suffers from ADHD, impulsive), considers her mothers' lesbian sexual orientation a disadvantage, and their family diversity as a nuisance and obstacle that sabotages her efforts to "be like everyone else." She entered first grade fearing the reactions of her surroundings, and to this day has a hard time "coming out of the closet" with her differences. The eldest daughter, on the other hand, is less concerned about the sexual orientation of the mothers and is not too shy to present her family, but has shown recent interest in knowing the identity of her donor:

Each of the girls is very different, there is... the whole lesbian thing – it's a topic that mainly comes up from Nala, the youngest daughter. It was never simple for her. Like she... she is also a very expressive child, she says what she feels... She went into first grade with a sense of: "When they find out I have two mothers, they might say something, and I'm different." Now, she's a different girl. She's a basketball player, she just rode to school on a unicycle, she obviously has ADHD from my side, and then that enters the picture, too. She just wants to be a little bit like everyone else in something, and we stuck her with this two-mom thing. It's a kind of issue that exists. For Nala – it bothers her. We went, she plays basketball, and we went to go see an important game, and my partner said, "I'm gonna come too, why not." Then Nala felt embarrassed, she said to me: "Mom, not everyone on the team knows that I have two moms." And... she thinks about it a lot, it's an issue for her. As for Leah, the oldest, it was always clear to her that she's the one who presents the family, and that's okay. She recently asked me if she could, if she could have any way of knowing who the donor was. It interests her. I told her no, that it's not possible in Israel.

According to Tiffany, it took her and her partner a while to realize that their children also face the constant burden of "coming out" with their family diversity to every teacher, instructor, class, group of children, or new friend they meet:

It took us a while to realize that our children, whenever they meet a new person, also have to "come out" every time. Every time all over again. And that was something that was really hard to accept at first. We didn't think about it initially either. It's something that took us a while to figure out, that every time they meet, especially when they were younger, now it's, like, easier for them, but every time they... each new classroom, new teacher, every friend we invite over or that invites them to their house, for them, it's like "coming out." And that's something that is... meaning, the weight of this is not only on us, but also on our children.

Careful attention to the narrator's accounts exposed the **"burden of proof" as an intergenerational experience** that often trickles down from the mothers to the children at a very young age. The "burden of proof" of children is expressed in two ways: 1) The pressure to excel academically and socially and be "special;" 2) The need to hide difficulties and weaknesses from the outside world (and often even from the mothers). The children seem to have internalized the idea that expressing any difficulty or weakness on their part constitutes a danger and a threat, since it can indicate poor parenting, which may be attributed to the non-normative status of their mothers.

Gabriella feels that her daughters have internalized a kind of model of excellence to prove the value of their lesbian mothers:

The girls understand that they need to excel. They need to be something special. It's like, we have this fitness trainer who comes twice a week to train us. Every time she comes, she comes at eight. At nine o'clock when she leaves, Hannah [the eldest daughter, A.P.] already set a table, made some things, cut a salad, arranged everything. She hears them, the girls: "I'll bring that to you, I'll take that back for you," and she is full of admiration: "What is this? What kind of girls are these?" It's part of... I won't settle for less than this. Now tell me, "am I bugging my girls?" "No." I say, there is some kind of model we're following here. After all, I didn't tell them, "You have to do this, get up and make a salad, if not, I'll slap you." But it could be that they, too, somehow realize that they need to be extra special. And they really do think they're something special. No one demanded this of me, but I wouldn't want people to say, "The lesbian's daughter, she does this and that." I mean, there's like a weak link here, so let's not let, let's not be the subject of people's gossip who go around looking for missteps. Now look, I'm not busy thinking about what people think of me all day, like I go about my day and don't stop to see what people are saying about me behind my back. But, it's there, there's nothing you can do. And they also have to... we all have to really excel!

Talia's words also echo the pressure placed on children of lesbian mothers to demonstrate resilience and excellence, similar to the pressure placed on the mothers themselves. On the one hand, their eldest son, Tom, presents himself in public in the same way that she and her partner do: Openly and with confidence, "nonchalant" to "everyone." On the other hand, his behavior at home indicates that his public persona is somewhat a "performance," displayed under the influence of the "burden of proof." Talia says:

All in all, Tom doesn't outwardly convey ambivalence or that he's dealing with hardships to other children or anyone else. He has self-confidence and about our family everywhere, at least according to what we see when we're out. He's not ashamed of anything. But in our home, he can cry about the fact that he really wants a father and we understand that he's lacking a male figure. By the way, after consulting with a psychologist, we brought him a teenage boy for a year and a half or two. We still have someone, he's on vacation now. He spends time with him, gives him some kind of role model, when it comes to male communication. You know, so that we won't miss anything...

Part of the "minority stress" experience for lesbian mothers is to keep silent about their difficulties and weaknesses, which seems to be the case for the children as well. Sharon said that when she and her partner watched a TV show about same-sex marriage with their children, and discussed the possibility of marrying each other, the son was happy, but the daughter panicked and responded, saying: "Oh no" and "we don't need to." Sharon and her partner's attempts to gauge whether the girl is ashamed of her family were met with "concrete" and a "wall." The child's therapist also couldn't get her to speak about her emotions:

> *There was something on TV recently about same-sex marriage. We sat in front of the TV and the two children were with us. So I tell them, "Oh, how wonderful, now Mom and I can get married." So the older one was happy, and the little one was like, "Mom, oh no." I said to her "Why, what's wrong?" – "We don't need to" I said to her, "Why, what's the problem, does it embarrass you?" and we were met with concrete, there was no way of speaking to her. I mean, you simply can't continue the conversation with her, "Forget it, I don't want to talk about it." My partner also tried later, even the next day, in elaborate ways to try and understand what it is about. A wall – the girl just won't talk. I also tried with our therapist, who is a lovely lady, she's studying special education, and she couldn't get through either. The girl is tough. I'm waiting for some time to pass and find the right time to bring this conversation up again.*

Similarly, Tiffany used the term "bunker" to describe their youngest son illustrating how he doesn't give his mothers the chance to get close to him or have an emotional dialogue about their family diversity or sexuality and love. According to her, there was a time when the topic really bothered him and his distress would be expressed in aggressive behavior and seclusion (not inviting friends over). Today he seems more relaxed and calm, plays sports, and finds comfort and support among his friends:

> *Otto, our son, lives in a harem of women. Even the cat is female... I think there was a time when it really bothered him. He had periods when he was very aggressive and very angry. Today he is much calmer. He plays a lot of sports and I think it really helps him keep his head straight. There are things he would never let us get close to. Everything related to... everything about girls, and relationships, and family, and that kind of stuff, he's not willing, like he's not willing to talk about these things with us at all. Um... unlike Sammy [the oldest daughter, A.P.] who definitely did share, who she liked and who she didn't like and we would have discussions. With him, it's a bunker, he doesn't... I know he talks to people, but not with us. He does with his friends. I think his friends are a very big support group for him. But there definitely was a period when he was much angrier than he is now. I think that now he's... something worked out in his brain. He's more comfortable in his own skin, in the context of... In the context of his whole family. I think we also see it in how he invites friends over a lot more and his friends come and hang out. It's like he's more at peace with the whole thing.*

In addition, the narrators indicated that the children faced incidents of rejection and social-emotional violence, both by educators and peer groups. Among these incidents are educators' unwillingness to introduce or give attention to the same-sex family, offensive comments from peers, speculation and spreading of rumors about the children's sexual identity, and more.

According to Audrey, the teacher of the eldest daughter's private kindergarten relayed his negative opinions about the idea of a family without a man or father, mainly through covert and non-verbal communication:

It was very difficult for Holly, our oldest. The topic of "having no father" was much more prominent with her. After she was in this private kindergarten, we realized that the teacher conveyed the message – "Too bad, you don't have a father. Too bad, you poor thing." How did we find out? we were there for Holly's birthday party, and the staff didn't introduce us, so we did it ourselves. The kids knew us, everyone, they'd been here many times, so it was nothing new. I saw the teacher's face, which was weird, I wasn't able to really understand his expression. Then, at the end of the party, I went up to him and said, "I sensed that you were uncomfortable, what, what was going through your mind?" and he wasn't ashamed to tell me: "She's a lovely girl, it's such a shame she doesn't have a father." I don't know how he conveyed the message to Holly, but it was so obvious. Kids understand. You don't have to say it in words.

At the same time, the children were exposed to instances of rejection and violence by their kindergarten and school peers, such as intrusive questions, offensive comments, and teasing. Toby mentioned incidents in which the eldest daughter came home from kindergarten and told her that the children were teasing her about not having a father, or claiming that her biological mother is her (real and only) mother:

The oldest one comes home from kindergarten, and it turns out that in kindergarten, even 3, 4, and 5 year olds tease her, "Mom, Avery said I don't have a father." Or "Mom, the kids said that my mom is Zara." "That's right, and you have two mothers, I'm your mom, too." "No, but Zara is my real mother." So I said to her, "Who said that to you? Who spoke to you?" and then she tells me, listing off the names of the children who said that to her.

In addition to the criticism and teasing about the different family structure they live in (two mothers/no father), there have been cases when the children have had to deal with their peers speculating and spreading rumors about their own sexual identity. Tiffany recounts such incidents:

"The older one had a period when she was about in 6th grade I think, where they spread a rumor about her that she was a lesbian herself. She was horrified by the idea," and similarly from Ramona's words: "Look, the girl came home a little while ago, saying she was told she was a lesbian, that her mothers are lesbians and that maybe she'll turn out to be a lesbian, too."

Evidence of "associative stigma" and "affiliated minority stress" among children in same-sex families can be found in the theoretical and research literature in the United States and Europe. King and Black (1999) examined the attitudes of college students in the United States towards lesbian women and their children. They found that the children also suffer from negative social labeling, albeit to a lesser extent than their mothers. Women expressed more willingness than men to be involved in relationships with children of lesbians. People who believed that homosexuality stemmed from controlled and environmental factors, showed less willingness than those with alternative views, to have a relationship or marry children of lesbians. In another study (Tasker and Golombok, 1995), young adults from lesbian families tended to recall more teasing from peers regarding their own sexual orientation than those from single heterosexual families. In addition, young adults from lesbian families tended to consider their own sexual orientation to a greater extent than younger adults from single heterosexual families.

At the same time, in Welsh's research (2011), we find strong echoes of the stress placed on children of lesbian families to demonstrate resilience, pride, and excellence, and to protect their families from any blame or defamation, all while self-silencing any weaknesses and difficulties. Welsh found that adolescents of parents in same-sex families in the United States "expressed feeling pressured to achieve, of being tokenized, and serving as a poster child for gay families – positions that may create a strain for all members of the family" (ibid., p. 66). Similarly, Clarke and Demetriou (2016) showed that older children of LGBTQ+ parents in England tended to be protective of their parents and hide any signs of difference or abnormality associated with their families. In addition, adolescents aged 12–16 who grew up in lesbian families in England reported a significantly lower likelihood of seeking support and assistance from the educational-therapeutic staff at school (teachers, teaching assistants, nurses, and educational counselors) compared to peers from heterosexual families (Rivers, et al. 2008).

In light of the mothers' experience of increased stress ("minority stress"), which included elements such as expectations of harm, pressure to serve as exemplars of normalcy and excellence, feelings of guilt and concerns about the consequences of fatherlessness, internalized homophobia and defensive coping strategies, it was not surprising to find that some narrators found it difficult to acknowledge that their children also carry the burden of "associative stigma" and face their own experience of increased stress ("affiliated minority stress"), and, accordingly, to offer them effective emotional support.

Analyzing the narratives, brought to light that the discourse between mothers and children tended to be informative and correct. That is, the narrators tended to provide information and explanations, and related less to emotional aspects. The narrators would often give the impression that they were providing their children with the same automatic and pre-rehearsed system of responses in different versions ("We are a family with two mothers," "There are all kinds of families"), without any regard for where the children are "here and now," and without necessarily adapting the responses to their changing needs.

Some of the narrators tried to present their children with an "edited" version of reality through various means: shining a spotlight on what they have and not what they lack ("We don't say: 'You don't have a father,' we say 'You have two mothers'"), as well altering texts in books and replacing a paternal figure with another maternal figure.

In other cases, the narrators tended to avoid discussing complex and problematic aspects of the children's experience, such as negative emotions (embarrassment, shame, anxiety, anger, blame), feelings of loneliness and abnormality, coping with stigma and homophobia, longing for a father figure, desiring to meet with the sperm donor, etc. So for example, questions of children like "What's gay and lesbian?" or "Will I also be gay or lesbian?" have been answered with dictionary definitions ("A lesbian woman is a woman who loves another woman") and "normalized" ("It's like a father who loves a mother," "Everyone chooses who to build a family with"), without engaging in meaningful discussion of the negative social stigma associated with these concepts, and without referring to the ambivalent emotional space these questions leave the children in.

Under such conditions, in which the existence of the father/sperm donor is denied or forbidden to be mentioned and addressed, and other complex aspects of coping with family diversity (such as negative emotions, experiences of abnormality and loneliness, incidents of violence and rejection as a result of stigma and homophobia) are not discussed or blatantly ignored, the children did not always sense a legitimacy in expressing difficulties, dilemmas, and distress, and sentenced themselves to "silencing" or alternatively, expressed their distress in behavioral forms (crying, seclusion, aggression, and the like).

According to Rose, the first time she and her partner realized that the girls did not feel a legitimacy to speak about certain topics, was when one of the girls mentioned the word "father" during a game, and her sister replied that they're "not allowed to talk about that." That incident caused them to change their attitude, initiate a conversation with their daughters about the father, and even get them to talk about their feelings, and make it easier for them to cope:

> *Leah, the older one, knew how to describe sperm donation at age six, and what happened, and it... really was very open. So it could be that with Leah, we, we made sure because she is the firstborn, we described it and explained it ahead of time, so it came from us. And then another little girl comes along, who even thinks about anything?! it's survival. The first time we encountered difficulties was, when they were little we heard them playing, my partner heard them playing in the room, and Nala, who is four years old, said to Leah, they were playing a game with a Playmobil set with a father character, and Leah said something to her about dad, and Nala said something to her like: "But we're not allowed to talk about it" or something like that. Then we realized that like maybe we had missed something. So we started raising the subject a little bit, to speak about it. So I remember on Family Day with Nala in kindergarten, kids aged four, five, singing all*

> *kinds of songs like one named "my father" and stuff like*
> *that, I was sitting in the back and asking her, "Tell me,*
> *does this matter to you? does it bother you that you don't*
> *have a father?" she told me "sometimes." And I told her,*
> *"Okay, it's important to know," and then after that, we*
> *also had all kinds of conversations from time to time.*

Ramona said that when her children raise questions about the
differences between their family and other families, they explain that they are a family with two mothers – a different family within a wide and diverse web of different families. When the
daughter shared with the mothers that children from her class
told her that she would be a lesbian, Ramona explained to her
what a lesbian woman is, and emphasized that it is a relationship just like any other:

> *If the children ask, then we explain to them that we*
> *actually have two mothers and that we are a different*
> *family. There are many, many families that are father-*
> *mother families or divorced families, and our family is*
> *different, too. Look, the girl came home a little while ago,*
> *saying she was told she was a lesbian, that her mothers are*
> *lesbians and that maybe she'll turn out to be a lesbian, too.*
> *So we explained to her – what does it mean to be a lesbian?*
> *it's essentially loving another woman. I mean... just like a*
> *dad loves a mom or like any other couple loves each other,*
> *so do we. That's what being a lesbian is.*

Ramona went on to confess that it took her a long time to realize that her eldest daughter, Julia, felt abnormal at a big school
where she was the only one being raised in a same-sex family,
and experienced shame and embarrassment over having two
lesbian mothers and no father. Ramona mistakenly concluded

from her daughter's silence that the subject did not bother her, but apparently the automatic and dry explanations "stifled" her experience, or she did not feel that she had the right to speak about the issue. Today, she and her partner try to get her to talk and share her feelings and experiences, but they are met with suspicion and partial cooperation:

And the truth is that Julia has to cope with this. She doesn't talk very much, apparently we're not enough, we... but we've been realizing in recent years that it's an issue. Just a little while ago she came to us and said, "You know what? it's not that embarrassing to have two mothers." And it was amazing because we didn't realize that she was dealing with it so much, with the fact that she has two mothers. And... and she doesn't have a father. I didn't feel like she was ashamed of us or anything. But it could be that she is, and we just didn't notice. Pretty early on she asked where dad was, if she had a dad. Really early on. We would explain to her that we chose to be, that I chose to be with Varda and live with her. It came up so early on that, like, later I don't think she asked anymore because it was really... it was already embedded in her, so it wasn't strange to her. Or maybe, you know, it remained strange to her but she didn't have the legitimacy, at least she didn't feel she had it. Look, I'm telling you that only in the last few years have I realized how much, you know... the moment I realized that Julia, I didn't realize it then, right? but Julia was like the only one. An only child, the only lesbian family in our community, until more people like that came, it really was wow. I said to myself, wow, the only child in an entire school that has two mothers. Um... but it's interesting, she copes with this. She has to deal with it. And we try to, like, speak with her a little bit about it. With some of the things, she cooperates, and with others, a little less. I guess our answers don't always satisfy her, but I guess she's gotten used to that... (smiling) So that's how it is. Maybe it came up very early on and all the explanations, you know, stifled her. And I could feel a little guilty about it... and maybe it satisfied her then and now not anymore, I don't know, but... it definitely preoccupies her. Definitely.

One can implicitly hear the pain in Ramona's words over the fact that her daughter felt the need to hide feelings of shame from her, as well as conflicts and doubts, about her family. In fact, there are several layers of pain here, all disturbing for the mother: There is the child's shame for being different, there is the mother's empathy for her child's shame, and there is the mother's painful awareness that her daughter felt the need to suffer in silence, so as not to cause her pain or damage the per-fect-family image.

And finally, Talia shared that she and her partner needed the help of a child psychologist to recognize the plight of their eldest son about not having a father, to show understanding, inclusion, and empathy, and to allow him to express his pain without fear-ing that "the world will fall apart." If before, the child felt that Talia and her partner were implying that "he can't talk about it," and that "they don't allow him to raise the subject," now the child feels he is allowed to express his difficulty to the mothers, and his crying and distress levels have significantly decreased:

Questions and difficulties arose with Tom... Tom [the eldest son, A.P.] was already aware from the beginning that he had no father. It was as if he understood much more at a very young age. By the time he was four, he would be on a playground and say directly, "There's mom, that's my mom, and I don't have a dad." He talked about all his stuff in the open. Like in a very... in a very confident way, he had no problem with it. We brought books from abroad, we would read books to him. Translate them for him. I don't think he even felt that it was any issue at first... and then when he got older and we moved here, the harder questions started up: "I want to have a father, a father is missing in my life, maybe you'll bring another man into the family, maybe you'll break up and each of will bring me a father. Maybe bring them and then I'll be in a family with a dad." We really talked it out and explained it to him. At some point we realized that he... the psychologist we were seeing, who we consulted with, helped us understand, we didn't come to this understanding alone, that he really just needed to talk it out and that we should let him, and not just give him answers. That we would accept what brings him pain. It's just really hard for him that he doesn't have a dad and he can talk about it and cry about it. And he would cry about it. Last year I remember how much he cried over not having a father. Me too, when I was little, I wanted... I wanted different things than what I had in my family and it was very hard, it was very painful. I can understand when it's hard for someone. And it really helped that he understood that we were allowing him to talk about it more. And also that... that it's totally fine that he wants a father, it's not something... the world didn't fall apart when he told us that. So every once in a while it comes up again like that, but not like it was back then, in the intensity of all the pain he probably had before that he didn't... when he felt that he couldn't cope or wasn't allowed enough to open the subject... when you realize that we're probably expressing to him that he can't talk about it.

Insitiutonalized discrimination against lesbian couples and parents, and socio-economic vulnerability

Multiple readings of the narratives using "The Listening Guide: A voice-centered relational method"[54] revealed that various forms of institutionalized discrimination regarding same-sex partnerships and same-sex families were a significant source of anger, resentment, and insult, and a major site of difficulty and coping. In addition to their inability to marry legally in the State of Israel, there were narrators who expressed resentment towards the State's (discriminatory and abusive) demand to undergo expensive, lengthy, and complex adoption procedures in order to be legally recognized as a non-biological mother to the spouse's children.

The arguments put forth by the narrators about adoption were twofold. One referred to the State's requirement to be involved in a formal adoption track, while any man whom the woman declares as father of her baby is automatically registered as such, without the need to prove his paternity, commitment to the mother, or parental qualifications (this is even the case with sperm donation). The second argument referred to the financial aspects (funds for filling out paperwork, attorney fees), bureaucratic aspects (long processing time, dealing with paperwork, working with lawyers, social workers, and judges), and the emotional aspects involved in these procedures (an experience of distrust from the State, and the need to pass "tests of parental competence" by supervisory institutions, such as welfare agencies and courts).

Jessie expressed displeasure with the discriminatory manner in which the State treats a female spouse of a woman who gave birth, vs. a male spouse, with regard to recognition of parenthood: While any man (with a penis) whom a woman declares to

---

54. Gilligan, et al., 2003; Gilligan and Eddy, 2017.

be the father of her baby is automatically registered in the Ministry of Interior records and receives immediate legal recognition as the "father" (without any requirement to prove a genetic-biological connection to the newborn baby, and regardless of the nature of the relationship between him and her), a woman (someone without a penis), who has a stable relationship with her partner, had accompanied her throughout pregnancy and birth, and is committed to raising the child with her in a same-sex family, is prevented from automatic recognition as a "mother," and is required to undergo a torturous obstacle course, carefully supervised by the State, in order to receive the desired parental recognition. According to Jessie, she had to wait two years before receiving the adoption orders for her girls. This interim period, until she received official State recognition as a mother, caused her great anguish and stress, and placed her in unpleasant situations (for example, when she took the girls to get vaccinated), in which she was required to provide explanations and justifications for her status and relationship to the girls:

> *This whole adoption thing is insane. There's something delusional about it, like it's so... I will never forget that moment. Upon leaving the hospital, when Olga was about to be discharged: "Name of mother" – they wrote it down, "Name of father"– what the fuck? if I had a penis, I could say "Jessie." Even if I had a penis, she would write down "Jessie" and... that would be it. We go to the Ministry of Interior, and like why? if I had a penis, would it be certain that the sperm that created this child came from that penis? like... every time I would tell people this, I would realize how insane it was. Beyond the fact that we have approval here, like adoption – come check our family and that's it. You ask me if the experience and work that straight women have to do is different? yes, it's different.*

When they're about to be discharged from the hospital, they say their partner's name – even if they're not married, mind you, and... that's it. And I had to wait two years for this moment of being discharged from the hospital and being recognized as a mother. Like it's... yes, it was very hard for me. Um... it was very non-trivial for me that from the moment the girls were born until I adopted them, I actually had no possession of them of any kind. I went with them to get all kinds of vaccines and things like that and I encountered situations where I had to explain who I was and what I was, etc. It was a very challenging time for me. I don't... I don't know if it's very rational in hindsight, but mentally, like, it really bothered me.

Hellen adds another dimension, according to which the adoption processes that are imposed on the same-sex family, while involving welfare and legal factors, preserve and validate its status as a "defective family" or a family at risk, in the public consciousness. It undermines the naturalness, value, and legitimacy of same-sex families, and perpetuates its inferior position compared to other families. According to her, when two adults want to be responsible for a child, and no one's rights have been violated, the State should not intervene. In fact, she and her partner are trying to find legal ways to fight their having to go through a new adoption process with the birth of every child:

The fact that our families in Israel have to go through the adoption process is something that really aggravates me and I think it's ... first of all, symbolically, it is untrue. Adoption comes from a place of lack, and our family doesn't lack anything. Families that were established in this way. And there's no abandonment, no death, none of these things, just choice and decision. Um... beyond that, the fact that we have to be at the mercy of some welfare officer and her cruel indifference is something that drives me mad. We did it with the older ones because we didn't have a choice. When our third son was born, we thought we were a stable enough family to insist on not doing this and to try and object a bit to the decision that this is the only way. On the other hand, it robs us of energy that is difficult to divert there now and of financial resources we do not have. So it moved pretty slowly, and we did end up applying for adoption after ... Most of the legal advisers we met with said that it was probably not the right time to start such revolutions. But it aggravates me. I don't even think this should be a matter of the State. As far as I'm concerned, if there are two adults who want to be responsible for a child, and no one's rights are being violated, then why is there even a question?

The gap between the external representation and manner vis-à-vis state authorities ("outward speech"), and the authentic identity and "real life" experiences can be gleaned from Adriana's words. Adriana spoke about how she is defined differently by every establishment (the National Insurance Institute, Ministry of Interior, workplace, etc.), such that the definition of her personal situation is variable, dependent on the establishment, and often detached from the real state of affairs at home. while she is running a joint household with her partner for many years, the Ministry of Interior defines her as "single," but she is not defined as such by the National Insurance Institute and her workplace. Even though she is raising three children, her ID card reads that she is a mother of two, because the adoption process for the third child has yet to be completed. In fact, without the option for same-sex couples to marry legally in Israel, and given the fact that she has to adopt each child separately, her ID card, which is supposed to serve as a document of identification and representation in her interaction with the outside world, not only does not reliably reflect her identity and the reality of her life, but also distorts and contorts them ("My ID is so unrepresentative of my life"). Although Adriana speaks in a half-cynical, half-joking tone, it is impossible not to feel the pain she expresses from the oppression and trampling of her authentic self, against the background of discrimination and disrespect by the State towards her choices and civil liberties:

> The "outward speech" is so strange that in almost every establishment we are defined differently. It's complicated when you have to explain every time answers to these simplistic questions: "Are you single?" come on, that depends who's asking (laughs): According to the National Insurance Institute – no, and according to the Ministry of Interior – yes, and at work – no... We have to explain it every time. "How many children do you have?" these are seemingly very simple questions. "How many children do you have?" now what do I answer? "The ones that appear on my ID card or the ones that are at home?" because it's not the same (laughs). It's very different. Right now, my daughter in first grade is learning what an ID card is. And I say my ID card is so unrepresentative of my life. I'm like single, I have two kids because I haven't... the whole adoption process with the third child hasn't been officiated yet. It's never true!

Coping with general external pressure conditions of oppression and discrimination on homophobic grounds, is one of the most prominent elements of Meyer's (1995, 2003) model. A 2001 international Amnesty International report indicates that people of different sexual orientations are the subject of widespread human rights violations, abuse, and mistreatment, ranging from violation of dignity to assault and murder. Many of these human rights violations are met with impunity, and are supported by governments and societies through formal means such as discriminatory laws, and informal means, such as prejudice and religious traditions (Meyer, 2003).

Legal and social contexts of heterosexism and homophobia have been found to be prominent agents when it came to the mental and physical health of gays and lesbians in general, and of women in same-sex families and their children in particular. Shapiro and colleagues (Shapiro, et al., 2009) showed that lesbian mothers living in the United States – a country where, in 2009, legal and social rights granted to citizens of different sexual orientations were more limited than in Canada – reported a higher number of family concerns regarding legal status and discrimination, and symptoms of depression, compared to lesbian mothers living in Canada. At the same time, children who grew up in the Netherlands in planned lesbian families, were found to be more open about their family structure, experienced less homophobia, and exhibited fewer emotional and behavioral issues than American children (Bos, et al., 2008).

Another general source of external pressure the narrators are exposed to as a lesbian couple, is the financial and social disadvantage, against the backdrop of gender inequality in the workforce, heterosexism, and chauvinism. In most cases, the narrators admitted that they were preoccupied with financial concerns, but only on issues which reinforced their similarity to other (heterosexual) mothers and families in Israel. Accordingly, the narrators described their financial stressors as part of the difficult economic reality that most young couples face in Israel, such as, high housing prices, high cost of living, turbulence and instability in various sectors of the job market, etc., while ignoring or denying any element of inequality, based on gender

(women) and sexuality (lesbian). The narrators' use of mechanisms of selection including "silencing" or "flattening" (Spector-Mersel, 2011) regarding issues such as financial problems
and social vulnerability, can be understood when taking into account that their desire to "normalize" themselves through their
narratives and show that they are capable of raising children in a
female family unit, without a man/breadwinning father.

Lily noted that for her, the hardest aspect of parenting is the
financial burden. She spoke of the financial burden in global
terms, that is, as a burden that every person who chooses to be
a parent feels, and carries on their shoulders (regardless of gender, sexual, ethnic, or other power relations). The universality of
which she speaks is reinforced when she switches from speaking in the feminine to speaking in the masculine:

> I think that for every parent, every person who chooses to
> be a parent, it's a specific type of slavery! you've taken on
> responsibility for many years to come and it's not just a
> matter of responsibility, it's also a crazy financial burden,
> um that of course, of course you pay for... I mean, it's not
> just...it's not just that your life gets harder, you also need
> more vacations and excursions, and you don't have the
> money for it. Meaning, if before, you both needed it less
> and had more money to do it, now you need it much more
> and don't have the money to do it. So for me, that's, that's
> the hardest aspect of all this, at this point in my life, the
> financial burden, not even the burden of care, but the
> financial burden.

However, there were a number of narrators who did talk about
the financial burden, while explicitly referring to the fact that
women in general, and lesbian women in particular, earn lower salaries than men. According to Nellie, the fact that a lesbian

couple is forced to live on two low salaries (the salaries of two women) is being "silenced," not only by heteronormative society but also by the gay community, which tries to hide any difficulty or problem in its pursuit of humanization and normalcy:

The process that happens from within the community is a process of humanization. We are one of the so-called "rainbow families." I think it's a problematic process. If I do it. And what does it require of us... it requires, it's being... I feel the silence more and less the ... I feel like the difficulties we face as lesbian women, are silenced. Statistically, female couples bring in very low incomes. Do you know what it costs me? All the "rainbow family" conferences. Each ticket costs about 25 dollars. Something crazy like that. And I wrote to them on their wall that this isn't a price that makes sense for most lesbian families. It makes a lot of sense for gay families. Certainly not for lesbian families. Maybe somehow for single women, but not always. It's an insane amount. It just goes to show that our needs as lesbian women are not heard in the community. It's true that the salary of lesbian families is low. It's two women's salaries. Women's salaries are lower on average, and lesbian salaries are even lower in my opinion. We need to check it out. But yes. Yes, and... there's also the issue of... There are many issues that exist only in women relationships.

In addition to experiencing vulnerability and disadvantages in their earning capacity, job security, and opportunities for advancement, the narrators' statements reveal their having to deal with phenomena of heterosexism, homophobia, and chauvinism in the workplace. According to Rachel, the fact that she is an "out-of-the-closet" lesbian boss at her workplace, does not prevent a co-worker, who is her subordinate, from making lesbophobic comments in her earshot:

> *I have "come out" at my workplace. But that doesn't stop people, mostly men, from making lesbophobic comments around me. One of my subordinates said that there is a lesbian couple in one of his children's kindergarten and that there was a family day at the kindergarten, and he said: "They were playing 'Tug of War' and those two lesbian beasts won eight times, they were both on one side of the rope..." Then he looks at me and says, "Oh, sorry." I think that it's inappropriate to call humans "beasts" in general, but that's who he is... He also speaks badly about gays in my presence, which doesn't seem strange to him. Even though I've told him a thousand times...*

Jane said that her partner, Daria, had to deal with machismo in her previous workplace, which was one of the factors that led her to search for a new job:

> *Daria is now actually starting to work somewhere new. She found herself working in a framework that didn't, that didn't really suit her people-wise. There was a lot of... machismo or at least some immaturity she experienced from the men she worked with. And mostly, she has a desire to advance financially.*

Evidence that people with different sexual orientations tend to face expressions of heterosexism and homophobia in the workplace can be found in Craig's research. According to Craig (1999), people with different sexual orientations reported dealing with direct expressions of heterosexism (sexist and homophobic jokes) and indirect expressions of heterosexism (assuming everyone was heterosexual) in the workplace. Experiencing direct and indirect realizations of heterosexism in the workplace was associated with psychological distress, health issues, and reduced satisfaction with certain aspects of the workplace. These results in themselves often led to regressive behaviors, absences, and thoughts about leaving.

Coping with rejection, violence, and discrimination by families of origin

In the "public-representative self-portrait," many narrators emphasized that they receive relative acceptance and sympathy from families of origin. This key message was conveyed by using mechanisms of selection of "inclusion" and "sharpening" events of acceptance and sympathy, on the one hand, and "silencing" and "flattening" events of rejection and discrimination, on the other (Spector-Mersel, 2011). It can be assumed that these descriptions helped narrators cope with key socio-cultural plots of pathologization and devaluation (Hequembourg, 2012), and served their need to defend themselves against cultural accusations of injustice and harm to the children's emotional and social development, due to their exposure to severe stigma, social ostracism, violence, and discrimination.[55]

At the same time, listening to the narratives according to "The Listening Guide: A voice-centered relational method"[56], revealed that the narrators' relationships with their families of origin were based on a difficult experience of trauma, suspicion, and mistrust, and were shaped by ongoing negotiations around normalcy, value, and legitimacy for themselves and their families throughout their lives.

---

55. Hequembourg, 2012; Kranz and Daniluk, 2002.
56. Gilligan and Eddy, 2017; Gilligan, et al., 2003.

The ambivalent and negative attitudes of families of origin toward sexual orientation, relationships, and same-sex families, as reflected in the narrators' narratives, were not expressed in physical violence or in any extreme ways. None of the narrators were expelled from their homes, physically assaulted, or disinherited. However, it was reflected in the use of social-emotional violence and the imposition of social and economic sanctions. The use of social-emotional violence is expressed in the following ways: a) silence and silencing, ostracism and alienation; b) shaming and blaming; c) devaluation and delegitimization – an attempt to harm the narrator's self-worth and influence her judgments and choices; d) power struggles.

The imposition of social and economic sanctions was reflected in the following ways: a) refraining from participating or limited participation in same-sex family life events (weddings, births, circumcision ceremonies); b) offering limited emotional, financial, and instrumental assistance; c) discriminatory and preferential treatment of biological grandchildren.

This attitude led the narrators, in some cases, to experience feelings of hurt, alienation, detachment, and lack of belonging towards members of the nuclear family, extended family, and/or friends of the parents. These feelings translated into the narrator having a poor and tenuous relationship (if any) with the families of origin and acquaintances of the parents, as well as the narrator, spouse, and children avoiding participation (or limited participation of only the narrator) in formal family events (weddings, circumcision ceremonies, Bar/Bat Mitzvahs, funerals, memorials) and informal family events (a family barbecue for Independence Day, for example).

Familyhood is a core value in Jewish Israeli society, and families of origin play a central role in individual life (Fogel-Bizhawi, 1999). Grandparents are an important resource, one that parents lean on, both for childcare help and financial support. Due to distancing and avoidance, the narrators are deprived of the privileges of having warm, intimate, and close contact with relatives and acquaintances: Affection, appreciation, approval, emotional support, social and professional networking, financial help, and more.

In quite a few cases, the narrators' "coming out of the closet" to the parents was accompanied by the parents locking themselves in their own "closet," through ostracizing and alienating the spouse, and the inability and/or unwillingness of the parents to tell about it to other family members, friends, colleagues, and acquaintances. Sometimes, the parents demanded that the narrators "return to the closet" and not tell other relatives. Even when members of the nuclear family, extended family, and friends of the parents figure out that the narrator was a lesbian (whether because they saw her with her partner and/or children at various events, or because they learned from a third party), they sometimes chose to cooperate with the parents in the silence and silencing, and ostracism and alienation, creating a situation in which "everyone knows, but nobody talks about it." This conveyed harsh messages of shame and blame to the narrators, forced them into loneliness and distance, and exacted a severe emotional toll on them, to the point of depression. Sometimes this silent relationship and silencing was terminated due to a formative event (such as the birth of the children), and sometimes it continued on for many years (even after the birth of the children).

According to Jessie, after revealing her sexual orientation, it was very difficult for her parents, especially her mother, to have a real conversation with her about the topic ("it's out there, like, they know, but it's not really spoken about," "a lot of tension," "we talk about it but we don't"). They forbade her for many years to tell her brother or grandmother about it, and to be seen in public with her partner. The concealment and silencing took a heavy emotional toll on her ("lots of anger, lots of frustration," "I was in a kind of depression"), and harmed her relationships with her brother and grandmother, an injury she is still paying the price for today ("I'm just coming back now from a weekend where I saw how bad my relationship with my brother is"). Only once the girls were born, and with the help of her psychologist, did the parents decide to tell her brother and grandmother, freeing her from the burden of the devastating "secret":

After I told my parents, they started a few years of neither here nor here, I mean... like it's "out there," like they "know," but it's not really spoken about. I'm, like, telling them, sharing. They immediately sent me to a psychologist. I sat there for a good few months talking about my girlfriend and all sorts of things. I wasn't treating it. I didn't really feel the need to treat it either, I didn't really understand what... I was already in a relationship with Olga and no... I wouldn't come with her to my parents, I would come alone. Grandma didn't know, she didn't know until the girls were born. It was obvious that they weren't telling their friends. My brother, who was 17 at the time, I don't know, something like that, a big boy, but as far as they were concerned, he wasn't allowed to know, "It will destroy him, it will break him, when he goes to the army, it will God forbid break him, it will destroy him." And then he got into a high-ranking course, so that wasn't the right time to tell him because it would ruin his course and then he became an officer. To make a long story short, it took about five or six years before I made it clear to them that it was between me and my brother and that, with all due respect, he was a big boy, he was already 21 by then, 22. And I told him and he took it very well, he didn't understand what the issue was all about. I tell you this with a heavy heart because

I'm just coming back now from a weekend where I saw how bad my relationship with my brother is. Especially since he got married and especially since he had children of his own and his whole outlook on education is, like, completely different. With my parents, this went on for many more years. My mom, every time I tried to bring up this subject with her and we had conversations, if you can call them that, it was always like, "I deal with things at my own pace, I can't be pushed." She accepts me, but she isn't able to come to terms with it. It took over a decade. It created some sort of "we talk about it but we don't" type behavior, a lot of tension, everything beneath the surface. When Olga and I moved in together, my parents didn't visit us very much. When the girls were born, I forced my parents to go public about it, because my brother got married and at the wedding I felt very detached, very... like, Olga was walking around there with a camera, like... to capture the event, I don't know, it was very, very difficult. I realized after the event just how hard this had been for me and that I was in some kind of depression. It really affected me in a very bad way. Lots of anger, lots of frustration. And I brought it up with my parents, I took them to my therapist at the time, I was in therapy, in multiple forms of therapy actually, over the years. From the moment that my grandmother actually knew, it opened it up completely, and from the moment the girls were born and they actually became grandparents, and the girls are the eldest of the grandchildren, from that moment on, they also loosened up. They just suddenly opened up like that. And it took time.

Heidi's words highlight expressions of silence, silencing, ostracism, and alienation from the families of origin, even after the children were born. Heidi shared that her mother, who passed away 15 years ago, did not get to know Olivia, her partner, until her last day. Her mother's lack of acceptance of Heidi's different sexual orientation manifested in the fact that she kept silent and hid the subject, completely ignoring the presence of the spouse ("She never said hello to her, never spoke to her"), and she tried to torpedo the financial assistance Heidi's father was offering them (beyond living in a large apartment owned by the family). Heidi's brothers also took part in the rejection, in ignoring them, and in boycotting the spouse. For 30 years, they refused to let her partner into their house, and when they met her at their father's house, they would treat her as though she was "air," "non-existent." In recent years, Heidi's middle brother changed his attitude and has been trying to get closer to them, but the younger brother remains entrenched in his hostile positions:

> My mother passed away 15 years ago. My mother and brothers didn't accept me at all. The only one who accepted me was my father – when it comes to ostracizing. It was very difficult for them. My mother refused to meet Olivia, she never said hello to her, never spoke to her. At first, Olivia would come to our house to sleep at my place, and my mother wouldn't acknowledge her at all. Later on, that stopped, too. I would go to sleep at her place. We would drive to Eilat to be together, 5 times a year we would be in Eilat. She didn't know, didn't know her, and didn't acknowledge her. My father says to me, "Oh my God, if your mother were alive, you wouldn't have children, would you?" so I told him, "Either I would have children and I wouldn't have a mother, or I wouldn't have children." Olivia says to me, "I don't think you would have children if your mother were alive. You'd be scared to death to have them." And maybe that's true, or maybe I really would have children but not a mother, because I

would cut off all contact with her, you never know. Even though she was a very good mother and very warm and very protective. But, in this regard, she was completely primitive. And she was very educated too, you hardly come across a woman this intelligent, but in this matter she was so primitive, to a crazy extent, "What would the neighbors say?" it turns out the neighbors knew all along, but they thought no one knew. They always made sure to hide it. And I always made sure to hide it, so as not to shock their worlds. My father was really the only one who always accepted us, and he would clash and quarrel with my mother, and there was a World War III between them because of me, literally World War III. He wanted me to move into this apartment, and she said, "over my dead body." He said, "Over your dead body, she will move into this house. She doesn't have to live in a small house just because you don't like that she lives with Olivia." There were wars between them over me. My brothers too, as wise and intelligent as they are um... this brought out how very primitive they are, they wouldn't agree to accept Olivia at all. She never stepped foot in their homes. When she would visit my father's house, they wouldn't say hello to her at all. They would really ignore her, as if she was air, as though she was non-existent. So, these are things that sink, that form, that stay. Today, my middle brother travels abroad with us and tries really hard to get closer to Olivia, even though Olivia has set boundaries and she's not very willing to accept it, she doesn't forgive him for the past. Olivia says, "I can't forgive him over 30 years, I can't, just because he suddenly found out that I'm not a monster, it's hard for me." My younger brother, I don't pay any attention to him at all, so it doesn't matter, I really don't pay any attention to him.

In light of her mother's and siblings' longstanding harassment over her sexual orientation and her marital and family choices, Heidi chose to distance herself from her family of origin and move away from her hometown to another city. In her current hometown, she feels free and safe, and her neighbors and friends are a supportive family-community system, serving as an alternative to the original family system:

> *Now, understand that my entire family lives in one place, and I'm the only one who lives outside that place. I don't want to live there. Here, where we live, I'm a lesbian, we're a lesbian couple, everyone's aware, everyone knows, it doesn't bother anyone, um... We are part of the whole experience here, it's like a small kibbutz, we are really part of this kibbutz experience. It's very family-oriented here, but it's my familyhood that I chose and I created and I established and I nurture. There, it was a familyhood that somehow abused my lesbianism for many years, it was very abusive.*

Another form of social-emotional violence perpetrated on the narrators by families of origin, was expressed in overt and covert "shaming" and accusations, such as disparaging looks, "not looking in the eyes," and talking behind the back, or alternatively, accusations, emotional blackmail, and threats. Zara described a weak and limited relationship with many of her brothers and sisters and extended family, amid experiences of rejection, blame, and shaming. The rejection, blame, and shaming that arise from her description are reflected both in explicit verbal communication (threats not to "come out of the closet" by the mother, lest she will kill the mother) and in covert nonverbal communication, revolving around the "look." For many years, she said, her siblings rarely made contact and "looked her in the eye," making her feel that they were ashamed of her. Even today, she rarely takes her daughters with her to formal family events (weddings, bar mitzvah ceremonies, etc.), because she wants to spare them the glances of extended family members, which she experiences as offensive that mock the "strange" and unusual family in their family environment.

The experience of rejection, blame, and shaming caused Zara not only to limit her appearance at family events, but also to seek help from her relatives as little as possible, unless she had no other choice. Given these conditions, any privileges derived from close relationships between family members (intimacy, emotional support, social and professional networking, and financial assistance) were denied to her, and the potential relationship between her daughters and her uncles and cousins is also significantly affected:

> *The person I had the hardest time "coming out" to was my mother. Because my mother was actually the most important to me. She's the most important person in my life. Except for Toby [A.P.] and the children. And I felt like I could actually do her harm, like causing her an early death. And it's also something that came up, because my brothers would tell me, "you're killing her." And today, it's my mother who actually accepts me, sometimes more than my brothers, who are younger and more modern than her. Really. It's hard for them to deal with this. They had periods where they even had a hard time looking me in the eye. Like that... Like they were ashamed of me or something like that. That's what they tried to convey to me, but over time, it blurred. I have all kinds of siblings. I have many brothers. So there are those who really don't, and there are those who... My older sister is actually fine, she accepts me and helps from time to time, if needed. Like*

she co-signed our rent, is a guarantee on our account, and... you know, she's, like, much more involved. I'm not really attached to my family. My family doesn't... it's only when, you know, I'm in a really, really tough place, if I need to, I'll turn to them. There's a part of the extended family that I don't feel comfortable with. Like, I have a bar mitzvah to go to today in the evening, and I prefer not to take the girls, because it's my brother's daughter who I barely see anyway, and all the ... for what? what do I need to stir things up for? I don't feel comfortable with all the glances they give us, "Here come those weirdos, the ones that don't belong, that... are not in the family." There are no others. We are the only ones. It's a huge family, you see, it can spread out to about two hundred people, and there's no one else. Just us. So why do they have to go through that? if... like if there's a choice, if there's an option, then we don't have to.

The social-emotional violence was also embodied in repeated attempts by families of origin to undermine the narrators' sense of self-worth and self-confidence, and to influence their judgments and choices. Arielle shared that while preparing for her wedding with her partner, her mother tried to dissuade her from getting married, claiming that her decision may stem from poor judgment, due to a head injury she had suffered in the past as a result of a car accident, and that after receiving appropriate treatment, she would make more "logical" choices:

I had a car accident some years ago and I lost consciousness and got hit in the head and suffered a head injury, which I only discovered later. But then, just before preparing for the wedding, I was diagnosed with a head injury and started treatment. Then my mom said something about

maybe the wedding should be postponed because after...
because maybe after the treatment I had, I wouldn't...
like the fact that I'm with Rene is part of my head injury,
and after my head injury is treated, then I won't really
want to marry her... Now these are things that are, like,
said during conversations, you know. She doesn't really
understand or doesn't want to understand the magnitude
of the significance of this terrible thing, this thing that she
just told me.

According to Toby, even after 12 years of living together with a partner/co-mother and two children, both her father and mother have not given up on their wish for their biological granddaughter to grow up with a father, and are trying to convince Toby to look for a man. Toby's father sees the creation of a same-sex family as proof of his daughter's failure to find a man and establish a "proper" (heterosexual) family, and blames her for that, noting possible flaws in her personality, such as arrogance, reluctance, and excessive pickiness, and pressures her to make changes in her thinking and behavior so she can find the right man ("Maybe, like, if you lower your expectations and your ego a little bit, it will work out for you?!"). Her mother accuses her of possibly harming her child, who is forced to live her life with the heavy deprivation of not having a father figure ("If you had Melanie with a man," "It's a shame she doesn't have a father") and tries to encourage her to find a man/father for her biological daughter:

To this day, my father, well not exactly, but more or less to
this day, he has pretty much stopped it, but he had many,
many questions like "Did you search deep within yourself,
did you find what was wrong with you? could it be that
you brought it upon yourself because you didn't succeed in

finding a man? maybe, like, if you lower your expectations and your ego a little bit, it will work out for you?!" even in the last few years, he had a little hope in his heart that I might be... if I had some desire within me, then, it may very well be possible. Why can't you? and to this day, my mother says: "If you had Melanie with a man," "It's a shame she doesn't have a father." It's something that they hope for in their hearts, that it will be, that it was... You know, both in past and future tense, but... their questions, you know, but with all due respect, they get answers accordingly, I'm not hiding or anything. I said to my father, "Men don't suit me, it's not for me! you've been living with my mother 50, soon 60 years. So... I don't want a man, I... no 'if's, no 'how's, and no 'maybe's, nothing, no! It's not for me and that's that!" (Sighs).

While narrators who are biological mothers were pressured by their parents to find a husband/father for their children, non-biological mothers were pressured to get pregnant and have biological children ("children of their own"), even in cases where they suffer from medical problems, and becoming pregnant could endanger their health and well-being. According to Jordan, the fact that she is raising a child in a same-sex family, that she gave birth to a premature baby and lost him, and that she suffers from a medical problem and will have to get special injections throughout her pregnancy, does not prevent her mother from pressuring her to have a biological child "of her own," which leads to fights and tensions between them:

I was the first to try to get pregnant. I tried for a year. I got pregnant, I gave birth prematurely at 27 weeks. We were in the NICU for two months and he passed away after two months. I had a cesarean section and you're not allowed to get pregnant for a year after a cesarean section. So we said, "Well, okay, we have another uterus." And Carmen [her partner, A.P.] managed to get pregnant immediately. Just like that. We flew abroad for two months, came back, and Carmen got pregnant, it turned out well. We found out what my problem was, I have a medical problem. I need to inject special injections during pregnancy. But that doesn't interest my mother. My mother has a thing with me giving birth, too. She really wants my biological child. I personally don't understand it. It led to terrible fights between us that I made worse, because I really don't understand it. As far as I'm concerned, I don't see the difference. And I would prefer Carmen to get pregnant again, also because of the circumstances that I'd have to have injections the whole pregnancy and things like that, so I don't see the point at all. So with my mom it actually came to a point where I tell her it won't happen just to annoy her.

Also, in quite a few cases, the parents of the biological mother (especially the grandmother) waged power struggles with the co-mother (the non-biological mother), while attempting to undermine her maternal status and parental authority, especially in matters of education and childcare. Legal adoption of the child by the non-biological mother did not always prevent these power struggles. Along with the feelings of pain and humiliation, these struggles created tensions between the spouses, causing the narrator to want to distance herself from the "controlling grandmother." Sometimes these power struggles stopped over time due to clear boundaries and realignment of expectations, or alternatively, with the help of family therapy, yet, sometimes they continued for many years.

Nora described how the relationship between her and her

partner's parents worsened, following the birth of the biological grandchild. The crisis in their relationship is manifested in her being ignored as a co-mother, labeling her as an "enemy" and "in the way," of the power struggles, and their attempts to control the child's care and education. Only after a while and after therapy did they learn to respect Nora's (legal) maternal status and parental authority:

> *In the beginning, when Omar was born, there was something... the whole pregnancy period and first year of Omar's life, there was a bit of a crisis between me and Maya's parents. Like, from the moment they even found out she was pregnant, they, like, only approached her with "congratulations," "how great," and like I was standing right there and there was like no connection between the fact that she was pregnant and the fact that I deserved a "congratulations." She's pregnant, but who am I anyway? from the moment she was pregnant, that's it—all they cared about was that their grandson was coming! and suddenly the very strong connection I had with them seemed to dissipate, and even when he was born, they were in a kind of crisis. They didn't know how to be grandparents to a child who had two mothers. As far as they were concerned, I was in the way, because there's the mother and there are the grandparents! there can't be another mother! if so, what would their role be, what would be their place? and the first year was very challenging. The first six months were very difficult, lots of fighting and shouting and really uncharacteristic things. Oh, a lot of anger, resentment... It got to a point where we went to a psychologist with them, so that someone objective and professional would make them understand that they were simply behaving inappropriately. Um, they just treated me like I was the*

"enemy"! they wouldn't let me... if I had to give medicine to the child – no way!! as if I was poisoning the child. The child is hot, the child is cold, the child's not hungry, the child is – they decided what I should be doing with him. Or... I had a cast on my arm for about three months out of the first six months, so they would always look me in the face with such sour faces every time I would pick up the boy with one hand, like, as though I was going to break their grandson in a second! oh, I didn't feel welcome at their home. Like, "bring the child and go!" like, "you're bothering us!" um, and then it passed... ever so slowly... We each learned to get out of each other's space a bit and... until they learned (sighed) to accept that... yes, he has two mothers. It's no longer – "Maya – is the mom," and "Nora – we're not so sure what she's doing here!" okay... it took a ton of time... at some point they started with, you know: "Here's Mama Nora, here's Mama Maya" and they got over it. Now they give me the respect I deserve and know very well... we taught them that they also have their limitations and up to a certain point, we determine things, we decide things, we are the mothers! and with all due respect, they are the grandparents and there are clear boundaries: what is allowed and what is not allowed. Sometimes, Maya's mother calls me with the child. So he says to me: "Am I allowed to have animal crackers? a little? can I have a little bit?" I know that he eats the whole package, but it's okay, the main thing is that they call me because she knows I don't like giving him things with artificial dyes. That's it.

According to Nina, it was the transition from being in a relationship to having a family that challenged her relationship with her partner's parents (the biological grandparents), especially with the partner's mother (the biological grand-mother). The biological grandmother's aggressive conduct is reflected in how she would "block Nina's path to the crib," ignore her (legal) maternal role, and speak about her biological grand-daughter only with her partner. Nina's deep pain and affliction can be felt when she burst into tears during the interview and had difficulty calming down. According to her, not only has the "appropriation" of the biological granddaughter and forceful interference of the grandmother in their lives not softened over the years, but they have become increasingly difficult (among others, due to the partner's weakness), and she has no choice but to constantly fight for her place and role as co-mother (vis-à-vis the grandmother, and sometimes even vis-à-vis the spouse):

> I'm just very straightforward about who I am, so for me, to decide to have a girl together – she's mine, and to this day, I am still fighting for my place. It's not that Mary's family doesn't accept me, they love me, but what can you do, they're not in the lesbian family experience, it's not obvious to them. I thought it would pass a bit over the years, but it turns out it's just harder because of the grandmother's involvement and this appropriation, it's not simple... (Nina bursts into tears, fights them back, apologizes, and gradually calms down.) Look, even when we would come home from work, there was a period where we would come back late, we were almost entirely dependent on Mary's parents since mine was abroad. They would pick up Annie [the biological granddaughter, A.P.] every day and I would come home from work and want to hold her. And she, her mother, would say: "Oh, no, go settle in first." I always say she's blocking my path to the crib. If they hear that Annie has a doctor's appointment, Mary would immediately receive a million phone calls. Not that I need that, I'm

*not looking for that dependency and anxiety, but I'm
fighting for my place. I mean, for example, anything they
ask about the girl, I'm talking about Mary's family now,
so usually the question is directed at Mary. And then, if
Mary doesn't pick up or she can't get enough information
from Mary, then she calls me. And my whole relationship
with her mother changed as soon as Mary gave birth to
Annie. Like, she turned into that anxious woman Mary
always told me about. I only was exposed to this side of her
after Mary gave birth. I mean, I didn't see it before. Before,
it was all laughter and friendliness.*

One of the most notable social sanctions the families of origin
imposed on the narrators was refraining from participating in
events in same-sex family life (wedding ceremonies, births, circumcision ceremonies, etc.) or participating partially (some relatives come but not all) or passively (family members attend but
do not take an active part in the ceremony and event). According
to Tara, while her family came to her and her partner's wedding,
the partner's family (the parents and brother) didn't attend the
ceremony, claiming that it "wasn't appropriate":

*After a while, Isabelle and I decided to get married and
have children. We had a ceremony, which bore no legal
meaning in the world, it's not something that gets written
down on the ID card that we're married. We still don't
have that in Israel, you know. It wasn't even a Toronto
marriage, it wasn't legal in Toronto then either. But we
had a ceremony, we had a ceremony, we had a wedding.
We invited friends, we had a wedding, as far as we're
concerned — we're married! the fact that it's not listed
on the ID card is a whole other thing, that's a technical
matter that's just stupid. We invited friends and family.*

> *My family came, Isabelle's family didn't... Her parents decided not to come. They don't have a big family... and... her parents didn't come. The brother didn't come, either. They decided not to come. They said it wasn't appropriate, sent a "congratulations" letter and some money.*

Arielle highlighted the importance of having a ceremony to institutionalize the same-sex partnership, with all its inherent complexity and problems, since it reveals where the parents and family members truly stand in the matter, often against their will ("If until now there were things that hadn't been said, well now they have become very, very clear"). It gives the couple an indication as to where they stand and what they are facing ("What happened here is that we suddenly understood what was going on about us in the family"). Specifically, some of the spouse's family did not show up. What's more, Arielle's grandparents refused to be present in the wedding, and her parents attended the ceremony but did not take an active part in it. Yet, the spouse's uncle pleasantly surprised them with sympathy and support, which they had not enjoyed before:

> *I think that a wedding is something important to do, to make some sort of, I don't know, event to institutionalize the partnership. Not for the couple, but for the family and the environment. Because what happened here is that we suddenly understood what was going on around us in the family. If until now there were things that hadn't been said, well now they have become very, very clear. For instance, there were people who just didn't show up. Like, Rene's family, whole sections just didn't show up. They didn't say they wouldn't come, no... they just didn't show up. My grandparents didn't come to the wedding. My mother came but she was more or less... like, there's*

one picture of her smiling in all the wedding photos.
We didn't know until the very last minute whether my
mother would come. So we decided that Rene's parents
would stand with us on the stage under the chuppah
and they spoke, too. And my parents didn't... And on
the other hand, there were also parts that were suddenly
like... like, Rene's uncle suddenly woke up... I don't know
what happened exactly, but since then, it's been a few
years since then, he hugs us and he loves us, he protects
us. And it wasn't like that before. It totally happened
because of the wedding stuff.

Meanwhile, Heidi described how her siblings denied her maternal status and for many years did not treat her non-biological children as her own. Her younger brother didn't bother to attend the circumcision of her (non-biological) son, and to this day ignores the concept of same-sex families. Her younger brother though, underwent a change for the better in his attitude and behavior:

In the beginning, my children weren't even mine,
according to my brothers. It wasn't something that was
even addressed at all, "The children are not even your
children." And my younger brother didn't show up at all
for the circumcision. He had a commitment that day, a
different commitment. Since they're not my children, he
didn't show up. No, my brothers didn't treat them at all
like my children. Today they are... my younger brother is
not a good example because I don't acknowledge him at
all in this matter, he's like a little boy who acts in spite. But
for my middle brother, my kids are really my kids, more
so mine than Olivia's, I think. With my middle brother,
they're really more my children than Olivia's...

In some cases, social sanctions by families of origin were reflected in low levels of interest and involvement, few visits, little to no financial support, and limited help with childcare. Zara said that her family deprived her of the benefits she would have received had she tied the knot with a man (wedding funding, dowry), and even punished her for choosing to tie the knot with a woman by not assisting her financially or helping her with childcare during the critical years:

> When I first told my mother and since I wasn't yet a mother myself, then maybe there was still room for change in her mind: "Okay, Toby is great, but maybe something will change in your mind and suddenly you'll realize you're making a mistake." But the moment I sealed the deal and there were children in the picture, she realized there was no turning back. We are a couple. Even though I didn't get all the perks I was supposed to get if I had come home with a man. Because they would have given me a fancy wedding and they would have helped me at home. But because I chose to live with a woman, I was punished anyway. A sort of punishment. A punishment of like, 'we're not gonna help you.' Okay, deal with it. Also financially. My sisters had a dowry and had a wedding. A wedding costs money. These days, weddings can reach 25,000 dollars, so I'm not getting married, so give me 25,000 dollars. What, I don't deserve it? "But if you don't get married, you don't deserve it." I know that if I marry Toby, it's like not getting married to her, so it doesn't matter to me anymore. I would marry Toby, but what, she'll say to me: "What, are you crazy? you want me to bring your uncles to see you marry a woman?" it's very difficult for us in this respect that we don't really have help. No one helps us as far as I'm concerned, no one helped. Today I don't need

them anymore, but during the critical years I felt like I had no one who could really help me. My mother is also older, I won't dump my children on her. Toby's mother is also older, so is her father. Nothing, we had no one. I see people around me. They have grandmothers and they can go for a weekend. We don't have it. We don't have weekends. We never had.

According to Isabelle (a non-biological mother of a 5-year-old girl and a 2-year-old girl in her early 40s), the transition to motherhood in a same-sex family was accompanied by strong opposition from her parents, which included total separation for a year and a half, followed by cautiously approaching them again. To this day, her parents see her as a "failure," their level of involvement in her family life is low, the relationship with her spouse and daughters is poor (Isabelle meets with her parents alone, for the most part), and the financial assistance they offer her is limited to gifts for the girls:

Maybe if I didn't have such a child-oriented partner, I wouldn't be a mother today. My parents were anti, they were very against it, after I informed them that Tara and I went through the whole process to get pregnant, there was a kind of separation of almost a year and a half... Yes... They were very anti: "That's crazy, a couple of girls having a child. That's out of the question, you're ruining your life! She forced you!" all types of "beautiful" statements like that. I'm combative by nature, so I told them: "Listen, I'm not willing to hear these statements. This was a joint decision. I realized that I don't want to live alone, and I want to continue living with Tara and I want children. I am asking you to stop saying these things." And that was it, then there was a deafening silence. At first, we would come every Friday for some kind of meal – Tara and me, and later, it suddenly became: "We don't want to see Tara in our house." Something really, really extreme. And as soon as my mother said that, I said, "If you don't want to see Tara, then you won't see me either" (lowering her voice). They are also very stubborn, also not so healthy. So after a year and a half, my mother softened a little... And on the other hand, I also realized that I couldn't go on in a state of war and in the end, if something happened, it would all be on my conscience. Um... and then there was some kind of instance of coming closer and Tara goes there from time to time. And I – on my day off, jump in there in the morning, usually without the kids and that. Now, I go a little more with the kids and Tara, but there was a very long period – years... that my parents... (lowers voice and goes silent)... I wouldn't have heard "bring the children" before. Now it comes up occasionally, you know, "bring the kids over once in a while" ... that really didn't happen before. Even when they were babies, my mother saw them as a nuisance, not something that was positive in any way. But now that they're a little older, especially Beth, and now she sees Nicole, too, who is very sweet – she gets smiles out of them – this girl, really – so, she sees that it's not what she thought before... They don't have any other grandchildren. My sister lives with them at home, she's two years older than me, which is a whole other situation, not the most ideal... So, as far as they were concerned, we're both failures, something along those lines... It's not just a feeling, it even came down to them saying things like, "We failed you," you know, all kinds of statements – what else can you conclude from that? what are we – a success? (giggles sheepishly)... Okay, it's a certain type of parent, it's a certain type of education and you can't change that. They help with what they can: they give gifts to the children... As far as I'm concerned, it's a tolerable status quo, and that's it. I have no demands from them, absolutely not... You want to help – help, you don't want to help – don't help... I... There are no requirements...

Another form of sanction is expressed in granting discriminatory and preferential treatment to biological grandchildren, compared to non-biological grandchildren. Nina described the differences in how her spouse's mother (the grandmother) treats her biological granddaughter compared to her non-biological granddaughter. While the biological granddaughter receives increased emotional attention (to the point of her intervening intrusively), the non-biological granddaughter receives a rather cold and businesslike attitude:

As a non-biological mother, I had to constantly fight for my place with Mary's parents. And I still fight to this day. And with Doreen [the non-biological granddaughter, A.P.], there is no comparison. It's not that Mary's mother doesn't love her... she loves her very much and accepts her, but there's no comparison here, that is, in terms of emotional involvement... it's not, they love her and everything, but they obviously don't have the same connection. They don't have the same relationship full of emotions, concern, and devotion like they have with Annie [the biological granddaughter, A.P.].

Studies from Israel and abroad confirm the abusive and discriminatory treatment often inflicted by families of origin towards women in planned same-sex families. Although the birth of a first grandchild and the transition of lesbian women to parenthood (especially biological parenthood) is usually a positive turning point in their relationship with their families of origin, and contributes to a renewed rapprochement between them and their parents,[57] lesbian mothers who turn to their families of origin for help and support, may experience criticism and rejection (Pies, 1990). Meir (2008) found that mothers in lesbian families (couples and singles) in Israel received less help from their families of origin in information, emotional support and financial assistance, compared to mothers in heterosexual families.

The National Lesbian Family Study in the United States found that only 29% of grandparents were "out of the closet" to relatives and friends about their grandchild's different family structure. Although this trend rose to 63% when the grandson turned five, only 14% recognized their daughter's partner as a co-mother (DeMino, et al., 2007). Also, family support for lesbian mothers is conditional and specific to the biological grandchild, and not necessarily accessible and available to the co-mother.[58] Grandparents are generally more in contact with the biological grandchildren than with the non-biological ones of the co-mother (Patterson, et al., 1998) and invest more effort in nurturing the relationship with the biological grandchildren compared with the non-biological ones (Hetherington, et al., 1999).

Coping with rejection, violence, and discrimination by the medical, educational, and social environment

In the dominant narratives of the public-representative self-portrait, narrators tended to emphasize the sympathy and social acceptance they received from the environment and society. Evidence of homophobia, stigma, and discrimination by the social environment generally underwent selection, including

---

57. Livni, 2004 [Hebrew]; DeMino, et al., 2007.

58. Fulcher, et al., 2002; Hetherington, et al., 1999; Patterson, et al., 1998.

"flattening" and "silencing" (Spector-Mersel,2011), that is, they were mentioned very briefly, if at all, while downplaying their importance and significance. Alternatively, if expressions of homophobia and discrimination were addressed by the social environment, they were often used as "raw material" to reposition the narrators as cultural heroines and agents of social change. However, careful listening to the narrators' accounts according to The Listening Guide: A voice-centered relational method[59], has shown that their relationships with the medical, educational, and social environments have been shaped under the dark shadow of heterosexism and homophobia.

Some of the narrators described incidents of social-emotional violence, rejection, and discrimination in their encounters with doctors and social workers in hospitals where they underwent fertility treatments and/or gave birth to their children. This social-emotional violence was reflected in attempts by doctors and therapists, people in positions of power and authority, on whom the narrators depended on for treatment or help, to undermine the mothers' self-esteem and self-confidence and interfere with their judgments and choices.

Toby described the ordeal she and her partner went through in the hospital where they started in vitro fertilization (IVF) treatments. According to Toby, the attending physician tried to dissuade her and her partner from their decision to have children from the same sperm donor, claiming that it would be doing the children an injustice and causing irreversible psychological damage, and even sent them to consult a psychologist. At the same time, he was "confused" about the sperm dose, and used another donor's sperm donation. Although Toby has no way of proving that he consciously and intentionally used a different sperm donor, she felt that she was vulnerable to abusive

---

59. Gilligan, et al., 2003; Gilligan and Eddy, 2017.

behavior by an influential doctor, based on unequal power relations and homophobia ("Apparently, everything led him to...
you know, 'let's screw over those two lesbians.'") In addition
to the doctor's homophobic and aggressive behavior, Toby reported experiencing lack of sympathy and alienation from the
attending nurses:

> And I remember we went to Hospital X, and we asked to have
> one donor for both of us, and the doctor I'm talking about,
> let's call him Doctor Y, sent us to a psychologist, to consult
> a psychologist, because in his opinion and to his claim, we
> are going to do a terrible injustice for our children, who have
> not yet been born, to have two mothers from the same donor,
> "How we deal with them and they with us will be very, very
> difficult, they will constantly be in a state of overachievement
> and will compare who is better, who is less good." All kinds
> of shocking homophobic statements, "You're going to do
> them an injustice, the kids will decide or see who's better
> and who's not." And he gave us a psychologist's card, "Go
> to a psychologist, consult with him about what harm you're
> going to do to your unborn children." I remember that we
> stayed, that we stayed for a treatment or two. During the
> second treatment, he declared that he had made a mistake
> in the dose of the sperm. After the treatment, as I was laying
> there with my legs spread apart, and Zara was at my head, he
> enters the room upset and says, "I'm sorry, I made a mistake,
> I got confused about the sperm dose, it's not your donor,
> what I used in his dose... We said, "You're kidding, right?"
> he wasn't kidding. Of course, I didn't process what had
> happened, and we fled from there as long as we still could to
> another hospital. "I'm sorry, I've never made a mistake like
> this." I said to him, "and this is the time to start? making a
> mistake with me?" apparently, it all led him to... you know,

"let's screw over those two lesbians." I have no idea, maybe it's subconscious, maybe it's conscious, I don't know... The nurses were also so antipathetic there, the whole place – anti. This is a place where, you know, you need the maximum amount of warmth and intimacy, and it wasn't there. We sat down to talk to him, and all the bimbos, the nurses, came into the room, the door was opening up like a revolving door and they came in, "Doctor, do you want this? doctor, do you need that?" and in between, you're able to weave in a word...

When Toby was asked to describe her emotional experience about the incident , she went into more detail about the feelings of shock, surprise, resentment, anger, and humiliation, from the attending physician's deviation from his role as an assistant in a medical-technical procedure, and his crude attempt to exploit his position of power as a physician, to influence her choices as an adult and to "educate" her, under the guise of concern for the welfare of the children:

We were shocked, we were shocked... The feeling was terrible, terrible. I come to you as an adult, by my own volition, I make the decisions – who are you to tell me that I will do an injustice to my children?! who put you in this place?! you have to check if all the results of my tests are okay, satisfactory, and more than that, provide me with the sperm I want in exchange for the money I give you, do what you have to do, get me pregnant, in the technical sense of the word, and send me home with a belly. Like, who are you that you... you are not my father, you are not my mother, you are not my teacher, you are nothing! we're doing business, just like when I go to the supermarket to buy milk and cheese, you have to provide me with the sperm that I need, that's all!

Nellie reported her and her partner experiencing misunderstanding, insensitivity, and lesbophobic humiliation at the hands of two therapists at a mental health treatment center for postpartum depression at the hospital where she gave birth. According to Nellie, the caregivers lacked understanding, knowledge, and tools for treating a female couple, were insensitive to the fact that the non-biological mother could also experience postpartum depression, and treated their relationship in a cynical and judgmental manner, instead of being empathetic and offering them support and guidance:

> *Serena was a girl who has very, very, very... she was a super difficult baby. Adam was hard too, but Serena... She had hypertonia. This means a baby who, from the age of zero, does not put her head down. Stress and muscle contractions. It was very hard to hold her. There was no sleeping. Nonstop crying... We love to go out, love to travel, and it was almost impossible. We couldn't travel with her. We were literally depressed for a year after giving birth. We even went for treatment. We went to Hospital Z for treatment, they literally have a mental health treatment center for postpartum depression that offers it basically to every mother. I gave birth in Hospital Z so we went there. It was a catastrophe. There were women, you know... and two couple therapists, too, there were also terrible and horrible and "put us down" and were cynical towards us, and they were really, really disgusting. I'm sure female couples don't come to them, it's not a common thing. There is also no understanding that the non-biological mother can also be depressed after childbirth. Like I'm talking about how bad I feel and they're playing with the baby... What kind of inclusion is that? it was horrible and awful. Then we called, we said, "We're not coming in anymore." So they*

said, "Why, why, let's talk about it?" (Laughs). No, it was awful. They also asked spiteful questions... let's say from the more marital side of things, all they cared to know was, "Was I a feminist before I met Raya or did I just get it from Raya?!" it's like they read into some kind of power dynamic that doesn't exist between Raya and me. Really, it doesn't exist... All they cared about was showing me how they thought Raya was controlling me. The audacity. Now, in retrospect, it could actually have been due to some level of lesbophobia, a lack of understanding of what women relationships are.

The attitude of the education system was complex and ambivalent. Alongside positive events, the narrators described incidents where they were exposed to humiliating, dismissive, and belittling treatment. Attempts from mothers to ask teachers to address the same-sex family in annual educational events such as Family Day or classes discussing the subject of "family ," were sometimes left unanswered, and even special requests for placement, taking into account how a particular class is made up, was often met with inflexibility and resistance, and required a prolonged struggle from the mothers.

The experience of many narrators was that they feel "transparent" in the education system, meaning that their families were not given recognition, acknowledgement, and legitimization in the curricula, and that their unique needs are not met appropriately. In the absence of a clear and binding policy on the part of the Ministry of Education, for better or for worse, they are at the mercy of every educator and educational framework, who act as they see fit.

Tara said that when she and her partner came to register their daughter in a private kindergarten in their hometown, and introduced themselves as spouses and as the girl's mothers, the kindergarten teacher "choked," "gave them the kindergarten brochure," "pushed them outside" and made every effort to keep them from entering her daycare. The kindergarten teacher's reaction left her and her partner in shock ("We got out of there, we were shocked!"), and forced them to look for another kindergarten for their daughter:

> I won't tell you that everyone loves us and that not everyone chokes... When we came, we were looking for a kindergarten for Beth, so there's one and one there, and we went to another place in the end. When I went in there with Isabelle, then the kindergarten teacher said to me, she said to Isabelle: "Who are you?" so Isabelle said to her: "We're partners, we are together." The kindergarten teacher choked and she just made every possible effort to keep us from entering the kindergarten. We said to her, "When is the registration?" and stuff, so she gave us the practical responses, while doing certain body language and gave us this kindergarten brochure, really pushing us out the door with it, "Make your decision and get back to me, make your decision and get back to me," that is, "Just get out of here, just don't be here." We got out of there, we were shocked! on the other hand, through a friend, by a stroke of luck, we came upon another kindergarten, which is considered to be excellent – the mother there is the manager, the kindergarten director is the mother of that same friend, a kindergarten running for 15 years, and they are incredible...

Toby described the agitated expression of the kindergarten teacher at the municipal kindergarten of their eldest child, Nadine ("She looked like she swallowed a frog") and the way her attitude changed toward her and her partner the moment they spoke openly about the girl living in a same-sex family. According to Toby, when she and her partner asked the kindergarten teacher to hold a discussion with the children about different types of families during Family Day, and to share with the children that their daughter lives in a same-sex family, they were met with even more agitated body language ("It really looked like she swallowed not a frog, but a whole chicken with its beak and feathers"), and with polite resistance from the teacher, "It's not part of the curriculum." Toby's use of figurative language with metaphors ("swallowed a frog," "swallowed a chicken with the beak and feathers") compares it to a picturesque and humorous situation, but there is no doubt that it hides deep feelings of pain and humiliation:

The people at the kindergarten knew all about us, but we didn't talk about it at first. When we met with Ren, Nadine's kindergarten teacher, she did some sort of evaluation of the girl's functioning and intelligence, based on all sorts of tests she had prepared. And we sat down with the results and she said, "I wish there were many kids like her, and she's amazing, and successful, and intelligent, and smart, and look at her spatial perception, and look at this, and she told her a story and asked her questions, and she answered so nicely, and this and that." And at some point we got into the topic of, "We're lesbians, we're an alternative family, we're raising her and her sister together." We put it there on the table... and... the kindergarten teacher... looked like she swallowed a frog... I remember it was around January, because February has Family Day. And we told her, "On Family Day, we remember from past years at the kindergarten, that there are family pictures posted outside. We're a different family, we want our picture to be outside too, for the kids to know. We want you to talk to the children about the fact that there are children from different families, that you explain to the children that there are alternative families, that a family is not just a father and a mother and a child." "Look," she told us, "it's not part of the curriculum." And then it really looked like she swallowed not a frog, but a whole chicken, with its beak and feathers. And then, we felt, both Zara [my spouse, A.P.] and I, that the kindergarten teacher's behavior and attitude toward us changed in some way. Again, from something intangible, which everyone is aware of but doesn't talk about, boom, she was hit in the face with our request that she recognize something different, alternative, that is not in the Ministry of Education's curriculum. Um... something in her attitude was different, something here changed.

Jade (a biological mother of a 7-year-old girl and a 5-year-old girl in her early 40s) brought up the unwillingness of the Education Department Director where they live, to comply with her and her partner's request to place their eldest daughter in the same class with another child who has a gay father, and who have been friends since they were born. According to Jade, the director objected to their request on the grounds that "it's not even a case, it's just an excuse." In the end, only after Jade contacted the school's supervisor, the counseling supervisor, and brought a letter from a psychologist to an appeals committee, did the director agree to grant her request:

Now we had a crazy story here when we were enrolling for school. There are two schools. There's a boy in Holly's kindergarten whose mother is straight and father is gay and lives with a partner, and they have been very, very good friends since age zero. They're very attached to one another, and also, you know, these are parents from the community, we meet them, which is something that really enriches our relationship and connection. And we asked to be in the same class since where we live, there are so few gay families. This is a school with a thousand children and there is not one single child with gay parents. So, like, to me this seems like such a legitimate request. And people here have come up with all kinds of stories to network their way into getting into the newer, smaller school... And well, we got the placements, and of course they're not at the same school. And I got so frustrated. I turned to the Education Department Director... In short, he didn't agree at all. He told me, "It's not even a case, it's just an excuse." He wasn't willing to discuss the matter at all. He told me, "If this is a serious case, then bring a letter from a psychologist to an appeals committee." Which I actually did. I brought a letter from a psychologist and said, "Listen, I'll go all the way to the Supreme Court with you if necessary. I'm not going to give up on this." And that's it, now it was a crazy saga. I went to the counseling supervisor, the school's supervisor, and everybody had to start bringing in letters as well, to also start explaining, you know, it was pretty exhausting and tiring. In the end, they approved it...

Jade went on to express frustration and outrage against the biased way the establishment treats lesbians; When it is convenient for the establishment, it treats it as something ordinary that does not require special attention (a "non-issue"), and when it is not, it treats it as a disease. But unlike diseases, lesbianism does not garner any empathy, desire to help, and mobilization. In any case, "it's never a variance that can be equivalent to the norm, but while respecting diversity all the same."

In other words, Jade expects the education system to treat children, living in same-sex families, like children living in normative families, but at the same time, is a different family framework that requires sensitivity and an appropriate response:

> And that's a whole other thing, like when they say, "It's not an issue." It's like a non-issue. Because if someone came and told me about a disease of, I don't know, that they want the child to be with another who has a similar disease, then everyone would immediately be overtaken with mercy, and if... after all, they always compare it to some kind of disease – "She's different too, she also has a skin disease, she's different too, she also has, I don't know, diabetes and they have to inject her." But when it comes to some kind of decision-making that requires some kind of sensitivity, then it's like lesbianism isn't... it doesn't stir up any kind of empathy. They put it in... when it's convenient, they categorize it as normal, and when it's convenient the other way, they categorize it as a disease. And it is never a variance that can be equivalent to the norm, but while respecting diversity all the same!

Some of the narrators reported dealing with incidents of rejection, violence, and discrimination from the social environment. These incidents included parents ignoring and forbidding their children to visit lesbian mothers' homes, homophobic insults from children and teenagers, intrusive questions and offensive comments from close friends, service providers and strangers on the street, and refusals by landlords to rent out their apartments to a female couple.

Toby described shaming practices and the blame she and her family are exposed to, from the children's parents at the kindergarten. According to Toby, there are parents in the eldest daughter's kindergarten, who turn their heads and do not say "hello" when they see her and her partner approaching. They also suspect that the parents of a very good friend of the eldest daughter, forbid her from visiting their home. Although the abusive behavior is not expressed literally, openly, and explicitly, Toby and her partner suspect that what lies behind it is fear of them being women who are labeled as "deviant" by society, and that this is their way of "voting":

> *Everywhere, in every society, in every thing and breath, there is homophobia. There are some people who... Like in the kindergarten, for example, in the kindergarten we are in today, there are those who don't say "hello" to us. You know, we would say "hello" to them at first, but then we stopped doing that. You know, I was taught that saying "hello" is basic, elementary. And... and... yes, you know, they ignore us like, they walk with their head like this (turning her head to the side). So okay, we don't need it... There are children who come to our house, Nadine's friends, um... There is one girl named Nira, who is Nadine's very, very good friend, her father wears a yarmulke, but her father is actually much nicer than her mother. And Nira never came over to our house, even though I spoke to her mother, and Zara spoke to her mother. It's probably like, you know, that we're "deviants" to her, it's their way of "voting."*

Following that incident, Toby described a brief exchange in which she painfully asked her partner if this was their fate and whether they would encounter more incidents in the near future where parents will not allow their child to visit them and their daughters at home, thinking they are sex deviants. Her partner answers her question in the affirmative, preparing her for the possibility that this is a lifelong struggle:

217

I asked Zara, with a lot of pain in my question, I asked her, "Tell me, this year in kindergarten, will there be many cases where we want child X to come to our house, and he won't because his parents think we're perverts and that we'll, God forbid, undress him and do indecent things to him, and teach him what it's like to be this way and that?!" and she said to me, "Yes, there will be, throughout our whole lives, there will be things like this." All right, you know, it's part of the learning. It's part of the coping.

Nora reported that boys in the neighborhood often shouted insults at her, such as "Lesbian! Lesbian!" sometimes she takes advantage of the situation to give them a history lesson about sexuality, and encourage them to rethink their attitudes toward homosexuals. She says she is busy re-educating the social environment "so that her son will have a better world to grow up in":

Look, take me for example... Kids from the neighborhood – sometimes I pass by and they shout at me: "Lesbian! Lesbian!" there's a ton of ignorance here. So sometimes I hear it and like... I don't pay it any attention, but the last time it happened, I looked and said, "Okay, I have fifteen minutes." I turned around, walked over with my dog, and said, "Who said that?" "What, no, what are you talking about? no one here said anything." "C'mon, okay, let's go, who's the one, who said it? at least be human and stand behind your words. I'm not ashamed of who I am. I mean, for me, it's not a curse. Do you want me to tell you where the word 'lesbian' even comes from?" I gave them a short history lesson about Lesbos, about Sappho, about... And they asked me with interest, "What, are you married to a woman? huh? and how did you get married? and how did you make a child?" I told them, "You can check online for

the term 'sperm bank.'" "Oh, of course, we know about it."
So I said, "Very good, so you know everything. And I pray
that if one of you finds out that he is attracted to boys and
will be gay in the future, I hope that he will feel comfortable
enough in his environment, that people won't tease him.
Because it's innate, we don't choose it, we only choose to
be real with ourselves." And that's it. Okay, they listened,
they were very into it and all that. Because I came and told
them, "Let me explain it to you," because they don't get
that lesson at home. it's important to me. Not for myself. I
am busy educating and teaching my environment, so that
my child will have a better world to grow up in.

We can understand from Toby's words that she faces suspicious attitudes and hurtful questions from close friends. Thus, for example, from the time the girls were born until today (four years), one of her close friends constantly bothers her with questions that doubt on her ability to love her non-biological daughter, and to feel the same level of attachment, commitment, and belonging that she feels (or at least is expected to feel) with her biological daughter:

Everyone always tends to ask questions, we have one
girlfriend, especially, who does this, "Oh, tell me, do you
love Nadine as much as you love Melanie? it can't be,
right?! how do you feel about her?" from the moment she
was born, I would hear, "Do you feel like she belongs to
you? do you feel a sense of belonging?" she is constantly
searching and asking about belonging. Now, the others do
it too, "How and what and where and who..."

Meanwhile, Nora spoke about the pressure the social environment exerts on her to have a biological child of her own.

According to Nora, once people realize that she is a non-biological mother to a child, even complete strangers in the park, on the street, or in a store, allow themselves to ask her intrusive questions and make offensive comments, such as: "What about you? don't you also want a child of your own?" which is based on the assumption that non-biological motherhood is not considered adequate, complete, and the same as biological motherhood.

The experience of "everyone's" constant persecution ("Everyone is everyone you can imagine," "Everyone is Israel!") and people's use of the words "Make one for **us** too" echo Berkowitz's (1999) claims, according to which motherhood in Israeli society is expropriated from the private body and the woman's personal experience and undergoes nationalization processes, such that the newborn baby is owned by the collective and not by the individual:

> *From the moment Omar was born, no one has stopped, sorry but yes, fucking with my head, and Maya's too. "Well, when is it Nora's turn? now you're up! c'mon, seriously, you don't want to? what, you don't want to? don't you also want a child of your own? don't you want to experience that?" and like... it's endless... all the time – "And what about you? now it's your turn! and come on, make one for us too!" and it's like... stop, I have a child! what do you want from me? like, if it were a straight woman, no one would be like chasing her around with... "Come on, make the next one." But because I didn't, like, physically (emphasizing 'physically') didn't have one, so everyone keeps getting involved in our private business, "C'mon, tell me, tell me, why not? when? come on, it'd be a shame for Omar..." "Everyone" is everyone you can imagine, it's everyone! it's Israel! everyone feels they can... It's someone sitting in the park, on the street, in the store!*

the moment they realize that, like, it wasn't me who gave birth to him, then right away... either because they know us or because they heard or they're the neighbors of... the friends of... that's everyone! The moment they realize it wasn't me, "Oh, okay, so then what? don't you want one?" and then like they're looking at me as if I'm still out of the ordinary! how can I, a woman, not want to experience it and not have done it myself?! or "Why didn't I do it earlier?!" like, they get very involved in the whole "why did she do it first and not you?" thing? and you didn't want to? and you don't want to?" and like, like... You're wasting our time, nosy people!

The experience of vulnerability and lack of protection became even more acute for the narrators who do not "pass" as straight women (cropped hair, leg hair), and/or for narrators with radical feminist agendas. Nellie described the street in terms of "a difficult place to walk" and a "war" area, where she usually doesn't have the upper hand. She feels that she and her partner are the subject of rumors and ridicule as "the weird lesbian couple with leg hair who ride buses." She also fails to protect her daughter on the street from sexist comments from acquaintances and strangers, that relate solely to her appearance. Her fear of being shouted at, argued with, and experiencing violence, causes her to avoid direct confrontations with people on the street and a deep feelings of helplessness:

We love being outside. We love to go out, love to travel. And, another thing we do is we're raising our children without a car. With buses. "We're the weird lesbian couple from the buses with the hairy legs and baby carriage," she laughs. I'm sure there are rumors going around about us... I wish it were a little easier for me to walk on the street.

It's very difficult for me. I have a girl... a beautiful girl. Like really and the whole world only pays any mind to that (smiling). To the point where people go, "What a gorgeous girl!" they don't even look at the person at all. Or they say, "Oh, you're cute too. You're also cute." It's awful and terrible. Today she was told five times, "Wow, what beautiful eyes you have." How do I raise a girl like that? I'm not the type of person to fight with people on the street. It's hard for me. I'm terribly afraid of violence. I... It's hard for me when people shout at me, it's hard when there's shouting next to me. If there's someone yelling and angry, I want to leave... So it's really hard for me to confront and protect my children from sexism on the street. Really, I'm not protecting them. Either I walk away or I shut up, and they look at me. It's hard. It's... at this level, it's a war. I mean, I work really hard on myself not to objectify them, not to hurt them, but on the street I can't get others to not do that to them. Not all mothers are committed to ideas such as touch, touch that is unpleasant, to educate the son to actually control his touch, not to touch women and girls, to ask. Not all mothers...

Sarah mentioned that while searching for an apartment, she and her partner came across a landlord who refused to rent his apartment to them, on the grounds that they were "a female couple." The feelings of insult and anger can be seen from Sarah's aggressive response to the landlord, "You know what? I wouldn't want to live here anyway!":

One time, we ran into an issue... When we were looking for an apartment, there was this place that we really wanted, and the landlord was both primitive and older, and he refused to give us the place under any circumstances... He said, "A house for a female couple." So I said, "You know what, I wouldn't want to live here anyway! (firmly)." And to my delight, we found a much better, much cheaper home. Apparently, we weren't supposed to live there...

Finally, Dori, a kindergarten teacher and daycare director, referred to how a mother of a girl who attends the same kindergarten as her daughter was interested in enrolling her younger daughter in her daycare, but did not do so in the end, because her husband refused to have their daughter in a daycare run by a lesbian kindergarten teacher. The difficult emotional experience she felt after the incident can only be learned indirectly from her nonverbal gestures (pausing, searching for the right words, clearing her throat) and her hostile declarations about her desire to "erase" him from her life:

The mother of a girl from Natalie's kindergarten [Dori's daughter, A.P.], whose sister, she wanted to enroll her sister in my daycare, she told me that her husband didn't want to let her in, because I'm a lesbian! um, um, (clearing her throat), I heard that and I said, "Wow! I don't want to see him..." Like, he doesn't interest me anymore! In that moment, he got erased. And there's something very homosexual about him. He's probably a homophobe!

Studies and surveys in the United States indicate that gays and lesbians tend to be disproportionately exposed to prejudice-related incidents, such as sexual assault, physical assault, robbery and property crimes, dismissal from work, discrimination in the workplace, etc. Gay and lesbian youth tend to be victims of homophobic prejudice even more than adults, and the psychological consequences of their victimization may be more severe (Meyer, 2003).

Mothers in lesbian families without a father (or a known sperm donor), tend to face incidents of rejection and violence due to a double stigma: The sexual orientation of the mothers and the fatherless family structure. Mothers in planned fatherless lesbian families in the United States reported receiving limited social support in general (DeMino, et al., 2007). A comparative study in the Netherlands (Bos and Hakvoort, 2007) showed that mothers in planned lesbian families, who had children through an anonymous sperm donor, tended to face stigma and incidents of violence and rejection in the social environment to a greater extent than mothers in lesbian families with a known sperm donor. Specifically, they were exposed to gossip and disturbing questions from people in their social environment, and described feelings of isolation and exclusion, to a greater extent.

Chapter 6

OUTLINE FOR RECOGNITION, EQUALITY, AND INCLUSION OF SAME-SEX FAMILIES

Conclusions and Recommendations

The narrators in this book are the first generation of lesbian women in Israel raising children in planned fatherless same-sex families. They do so in a socio-political environment where their community of LGBTQ+ suffers from prejudice, violence, and discrimination, and fights for legitimacy and equal rights. Their historic, pioneering, and unprecedented position, largely shaped the way they articulated their narrative identity and gave meaning to their life experiences and motherhood.

The stories the book presents, shed light on these brave and trailblazing women who face a double social stigma – stigma about their sexual orientation and stigma about not having a father in the family. The **"burden of proof,"** that is, the pressure to "prove" to the heterosexual society that they can raise healthy, normal children in such a controversial family constellation, lays the foundation for "representative parenting," yet at the same time proved to be one of the most significant sources of mental stress in their "minority stress" experience.

Their stories indicate that their children share some of the difficulties, stressors, and challenges with their mothers, although generally with less intensity and frequency. The experience of "minority stress" in general, and of "burden of proof" in particular, was found to be an **intergenerational experience**, expressed in how the children feel the need to demonstrate resilience, joy, and pride in their family and to function exceptionally in all areas of their life in order to testify to the normalcy and parental competence of their mothers. In this sense, it can be said that children face **"associative stigma"** (Goffman, 1963) and **"affiliated minority stress"** (a term I propose to describe the children's experience of stress).

Listening to the narratives sheds new light on the question posed by Meyer (2016): "How do apparent changes in the social environment affect the lived experience of LGBT?"

We learn that the "minority stress" experience does not disappear or dissipate under conditions of an improved social environment, but takes on new configurations and expressions, such as, the need to demonstrate parenting excellence, hypervigilance, information management, and standing ones guard, the pressure to raise children who are simultaneously special and normal (i.e., heterosexual and cisgender), and the pressure to serve as a model and source of support for the LGBTQ+ community. In fact, the "minority stress" experience continues to be an integral and essential element in the lives of same-sex families, and distinguishes them from heterosexual families (rather than any flaw in same-sex parenting).

The women's accounts confirm how the effects of institutionalized and prolonged oppression on subjectivity, are perceived in terms of "insidious trauma." "Insidious trauma," a term coined by Root (1992), is continuous social trauma that is based on invisibility and symbolic control. It is not characterized by actual life danger but rather by a constant threat to the "self," and its psychological manifestations are shame, guilt and damage to one's self-worth. Under such conditions of constant existential threat, there is a constant need for the "self" to employ emergency mechanisms, such as vigilance and preparedness, as a permanent way to regulate the experience. The "insidious trauma" model originates from the premise that the "deterioration" occurs in the social reality, and demands a psychopolitical conception of recovery – which encourages the individual to take on a reflexive, critical, and political position, and at the same time requires a change in external social conditions (Ziv, 2012).

Under such stressful conditions, as they are reflected in these stories, it is difficult to talk about the transition of lesbian women in Israel to motherhood and family life in terms of "returning home" to the comfortable and pleasant bosom of heterosexual society. It would probably be more accurate to refer to this transition in concepts such as "hybridity" and "the third space" as put forth by Bhabha (Bhabha, 1990, 1994) or "borderlands" as suggested by Anzaldúa (2012), to describe a crossroads of cultures, a site of contradictions, a space of negotiation and translation of social identities, in a period of historical transformation.

Despite the relatively privileged background of the women narrators in this book, the split in identity they experience can be characterized by paraphrasing the imagery "black skin, white masks" (Fanon, 2008). Fanon used this image to describe the internal crisis experienced by black people who are subjected to the reinitiation of white colonial people and try to be like them. These relationships largely echo the experience of fragmentation, as reflected in this book, among lesbian women who are subjected to normalization processes due to the transition to motherhood and family, and who try to simultaneously imitate and surpass heterosexual motherhood. The internalization of the "heteronormative and heterosexist view" in the context of social trauma (insidious trauma), creates pressure for them to be role models and examples of normalcy and excellence, and raise their children according to heteronormative standards of sexuality and gender (**"heteronormative masks"**), while subordinating and suppressing queer and alternative aspects of identity (**"queer skin"**). The relentless pursuit of a valued, central identity that will never be fully attainable, while silencing and blurring queer "otherness," translates into feelings of fragmentation, falsehood, and self-alienation, and imprisons their identity in an infinite hybrid space of **"becoming"** a normal and respectable person, in a society where heterosexuality is a standard for normality and worth.

Recommendations for Policymakers, Educators, and Practitioners

The oppression and suffering of lesbian families is generally not understood and recognized in Israeli society as well as in many other countries around the world. The lack of recognition, the opacity, and failure to receive appropriate responses to their unique difficulties and needs, were revealed as an additional external source of stress for mothers, and a site of struggle and coping. In this sense, the stories in this book contribute to the knowledge about the interrelationship between social stigma and mental health among minorities, and to raising awareness of the increased stress experienced in primary same-sex fatherless families by the mothers and their children. They indicate the urgent need for change and intervention, both from legislators, decision makers, and policy makers; and from educators and therapists.

Legislators, decision makers, and public policy makers should examine how social conditions in their country can be altered so that same-sex families receive recognition, social acceptance, and legal rights. With recognition and equality, lesbian families will be less exposed to prejudice, rejection, and violence and will enjoy mental well-being and a better quality of life. For example, it is vital to examine how same-sex partnerships and families can receive full legal recognition and equal rights in all countries an communities and ensure that these rights are preserved and enforced. It is imperative that non-biological mothers immediately and automatically receive full legal recognition of their parenthood. In addition, it is recommended to expand existing programs in Israel and other countries to include sperm donation from known donors, for women and children in lesbian families who wish to be in contact with the donor.

Furthermore, educators and therapists can use the findings in this book to learn about the experiences of women and children in planned fatherless lesbian families, to understand the unique difficulties, stressors, and challenges they face, and to offer them more tailored and accurate aid. Among the recommendations that the education system and teaching staff can adopt are the following:

- The Ministry of Education should draft a clear policy for educators and teaching staff on the attitudes and treatment of children in same-sex families, and present detailed protocols on how to work with the children and parents.
- It is imperative that the teaching staff undergo training and education on topics of gender, sexual orientation, and children in same-sex families. It is recommended to train and appoint one of the members of the educational staff (an educator, educational counselor, inclusion teacher, etc.) to the position of school coordinator on issues of gender, sexuality, and same-sex families.
- It is important to include people among the management and educational staff with different gender identities and "out of the closet" sexual orientations, who live in diverse families.
- It is important to empower parents from diverse families and to allow for their representation and expression on various

leadership and decision-making platforms in the educational institution (such as an institutional parents' committee, etc.).

- The subject of same-sex families should be included in the formal state education curricula, in various subjects such as, citizenship, geography, history, literature, social sciences, life skills, as well as in various contexts: "Family Day," "International Women's Day," "International Day Against Homophobia, Transphobia and Biphobia," and others.

- Management staff and teachers should examine ways to present same-sex family life in the educational setting, and grant it recognition and legitimacy, for example, by displaying pictures, songs, stories, and representations of same-sex families in classrooms and school hallways, displaying pride flags and pride symbols in the principal's office and counselor's room, adding books about diverse families to school libraries, etc.

- It is essential to invite experts and LGBTQ+ community organizations to lecture on topics of sexual orientation, gender, and same-sex families, both for the educational staff and for all parents.

- It is important to use discretion when assigning a homeroom teacher to a classroom with a child from a same-sex family, so the teacher will display tolerant attitudes, knowledge, and appropriate tools.

- It is recommended to take into account the unique requests of parents on their child's placement in classes with specific children (for example, placement in the same class with another familiar child from a same-sex or alternative family). This placement can alleviate the child's loneliness and abnormality felt by children and their parents.

- Transitions between educational frameworks (from kindergarten to elementary school, from elementary school to middle school and high school) constitute stressful and dangerous situations for children and mothers in same-sex families, due to the need to "come out" again and the fear of offensive reactions. Educators should be aware of this difficulty and use this point of transition as an opportunity to meet the same-sex families.

- It is essential that every educator devote time and attention to getting to know the same-sex family, clarifying needs, and coordinating expectations.
- It is imperative to create a safe and secure space for children in same-sex families and their parents, and to clearly and stubbornly combat homophobic bullying and violence.
- If necessary, tailored programs should be developed for children in same-sex families (together with therapeutic bodies), that takes into account the variety of stressors, difficulties, and unique challenges they and their families face.

Among the recommendations that can be implemented by the Ministry of Welfare and Social Affairs, the Ministry of Health, social workers, psychologists, and therapists are the following:

- The Ministry of Welfare and Social Affairs and the Ministry of Health should train social workers and family therapists and equip them with knowledge and effective tools for working with mothers and children in same-sex families.
- Under conditions where mothers are required to demonstrate normalcy and excellence, they may find it difficult to recognize their children's experience of increased stress and allow them to express difficulties and weaknesses. The children might feel pressured to hide distress and conflicts from their mothers in order to protect the family. It is important for social workers and caregivers to be aware of that and help mothers and children overcome these obstacles, in order to build relationships that are based on open, meaningful, and quality communication.

- The relationship between mothers and children in planned fatherless same-sex families and their families of origin is complex and vulnerable. In Israel, as well as in many other countries around the world, family is a core value, and families of origin have an important place in their lives. Customized treatment programs on individual, relationship, and family levels can assist mothers and their children in rehabilitating relationships with families of origin and strengthening the same-sex families themselves.
- The experience of increased stress of mothers and children in lesbian families is a multidimensional experience, consisting of both internal and external sources of stress. Therefore, any treatment plan should address the totality of these sources. Special attention and sensitivity should be given to the fact that part of the experience of rejection and discrimination to which mothers and their children are exposed to, is based on invisible symbolic acts, and on social-emotional violence.
- Vigilance, standing guard, and the tendency to show outward resilience are part of lesbian families' defensive coping patterns in the current socio-political context. Accordingly, each intervention plan offered to mothers and/or their children, should be adapted to their pace, characteristics, and unique needs.

References

- Allport, Gordon Williard, 1954. *The Nature of Prejudice*, Cambridge Mass: Addison-Wesley Publishing Company.
- Beals, Kristin P., Peplau, Letitla A., and Gable, Shelly L., 2009. "Stigma management and well-being: The role of perceived social support, emotional processing and suppression," *Personality & Social Psychology Bulletin* 35(7): 867-879.
- Ben-Ari, Adital, 2001a. "Homosexuality and heterosexism: Views from academics in the helping professions," *British Journal of Social Work* 31: 119-131.
  – 2001b. "Changes and developments in homosexuality research: A three decade perspective," *The Journal of Applied Social Sciences* 25(2): 169- 174.
- Ben-Ari, Adital, and Efrat, Rivi, 2002. "Narratives of Israeli lesbian adolescents' coming out: The dialectic between experiences of marginality and mainstream conformity," *Arête* 26: 46-56.
- Ben-Ari, Adital, and Livni, Tali, 2006. "Motherhood is not a given thing: Experiences and constructed meanings of biological and nonbiological lesbian mothers," *Sex Roles* 54: 521-531.
- Ben-Ari, Adital, and Weinberg-Kurnik, Galia, 2007. "The dialectics between the personal and the interpersonal in the experiences of adoptive single mothers by choice," *Sex Roles* 56: 823-833.
- Bhabha, Homi K., 1990. "The third space – Interview with Homi Bhabha," in: *Identity: Community, Culture, Difference*, ed. Jonathan Rutherford, London: Lawrence and Wishart, pp. 207-221. – 1994. *The Location of Culture*, London: Routledge.
- Bos, Henny M.W., Van Balen Frank, Van Den Boom, Dymphna C., and Sandfort, Theodorus G.M., 2004. "Minority stress, experience of parenthood and child adjustment in lesbian families," *Journal of Reproductive and Infant psychology* 22(4): 291-305.
- Bos, Henny M.W., Van Balen, Frank., and Van Den Boom, Dymphna C., 2005. "Lesbian families and family function: An overview," *Patient, Education & Counseling* 59: 263-275.
- Bos, Henny M.W., and Hakvoort, Esther M., 2007. "Child adjustment and parenting in planned lesbian families with known and as-yet unknown donors," *Journal of Psychosomatic Obstetrics & Gynecology* 28(2): 121- 129.

- Bos, Henny M.W., Van Balen, Frank, Gartrell, Nanette K., Peyser, Heidi, and Sandfort, Theodorus G.M., 2008. "Children in planned lesbian families: A cross-cultural comparison between the United States and the Netherlands," *American Journal of Orthopsychiatry* 78(2): 211-219.
- Brown, Lyn Mikel, and Gilligan, Carol, 1992. "The harmonics of relationship." in: *Meeting at the Crossroads: Women's Psychology and Girls' Development*, eds. Lyn Mikel Brown and Carol Gilligan, Cambridge: Harvard University Press, pp. 18-41.
- Chodorow, Nancy, 1999, *The Reproduction of Motherhood: Psychoanalysis and the Sociology of Gender*, Berkeley and Los-Angeles: University of California Press.
- Clarke, Victoria, 2002. "Resistance and normalization in the construction of lesbian and gay families: A discursive analysis," in: *Lesbian and Gay Psychology*: New Perspectives, eds. Adrian Coyle and Celia Kitzinger, Oxford: Blackwell, pp. 98-116.
  – 2008. "From outsiders to motherhood to reinventing the family: Constructions of lesbian parenting in the psychological literature – 1886- 2006," *Women's Studies International Forum* 31(2): 118-128.
- Clarke, Victoria, and Demetriou, Eleni, 2016. "Not a big deal? Exploring the accounts of adult children of lesbian, gay and trans parents," *Psychology and Sexuality* 7(2): 131-148.
- Clarke, Victoria, and Kitzinger, Celia, 2004. "Lesbian and gay parents on talk shows: Resistance or collusion in heterosexism?" *Qualitative Research in Psychology* 1: 195-217.
- Craig, Waldo R., 1999. "Working in a majority context: A structural model of heterosexism as minority stress in the workplace." *Journal of Counseling Psychology* 46(2): 218-232.
- De Medeiros, Kate, 2005. "The complementary self: Multiple perspectives on the aging person," *Journal of Aging Studies* 19: 1-13.
- DeMino, Kathleen A., Appleby, George, and Fisk, Deborah, 2007. "Lesbian mothers with planned families: A comparative study of internalized homophobia and social support," *American Journal of Orthopsychiatry* 77(1): 165-173.
- DiLapi, Elena Marie, 1989. "Lesbian mothers and the motherhood hierarchy," *Journal of Homosexuality* 18 (1-2): 101-121.
- DiQuinzio, Patrice, 1999. *The Impossibility of Motherhood: Feminism, Individualism, and the Problem of Mothering*, New York: Routledge.
- Duggan, Lisa, 2003, *The twilight of equality? Neoliberalism, cultural politics, and the attack on democracy*, Boston, MA: Beacon Press.
- Esterberg, Kristin G., 2008. "Planned parenthood: The construction of motherhood in lesbian mother advice books." in: *Feminist Mothering*, ed. Andrea O'Reilly, Albany: State University of New York Press,

pp. 75-88. Flores, Andrew R., 2014. *National trends in public opinion on LGBT Rights in the United States*, Los Angeles, CA: The Williams Institute, UCLA School of Law.

- Fulcher, Megan, Chan, Raymond W., Raboy, Barbara, and Patterson, Charlotte J., 2002. "Contact With Grandparents Among Children Conceived Via Donor Insemination by Lesbian and Heterosexual Mothers." *Parenting: Science and Practice* 2(1): 61-76.
- Gabb, Jacqui, 2004. "Imag(in)ing the queer lesbian family," in: *Mother Outlaws – Theories and Practices of Empowered Mothering*, ed. Andrea O'Reilly, Toronto: Women's Press, pp. 123-130.
- Gartrell, Nanette K., and Bos, Henny M.W., 2010. "US national longitudinal lesbian family study: psychological adjustment of 17-year-old adolescents." *Pediatrics* 126(1): 28-36.
- Gartrell, Nanette K., Bos, Henny M.W., and Goldberg, Naomi G, 2011. "Adolescents of the U.S. national longitudinal lesbian family study: Sexual orientation, sexual behavior and sexual risk exposure," *Archives of Sexual Behavior* 40: 1199-1209.
- Gates, Gary J, 2015. "Marriage and family: LGBT individuals and same-sex couples," *Future of Children* 25(2): 67-87.
- Gilligan, Carol, 1990. "Joining the resistance: Psychology, politics, girls and women," *Michigan Quarterly Review*, 255-297.
- Gilligan, Crol, and Eddy, Jessica, 2017. "Listening as a path to psychological discovery": An introduction to the listening guide," *Perspectives on Medical Education* 6(2): 76-81.
- Gilligan, Carrol, Spencer, Renee, Weinberg, Katherine, and Bertsch, Tatiana, 2003. "On the listening guide: A voice-centered relational method," in: *Qualitative Research in Psychology: Expanding Perspectives in Methodology and Design*, eds. Paul Camic, Jean Rhodes, and Lucy Yardley, Washington, D.C: American Psychological Association, pp. 157-172.
- Goffman, Erving, 1963. *Stigma: Notes on the Management of Spoiled Identity*. Englewood Cliffs, NJ: Prentice Hall.
- Golombok, Susan, Tasker, Fiona, and Murray, Clare, 1997. "Children Raised in Fatherless Families from Infancy: Family Relationships and the Socioemotional Development of Children of Lesbian and Single Heterosexual Mothers," *Journal of child psychology and psychiatry* 38(7): 783-791.
- Golombok, Susan, and Badger, Shirlene, 2010. "Children raised in mother-headed families from infancy: A follow-up of children of lesbian and single heterosexual mothers, at early adulthood," *Human Reproductions,* 25(1(: 150-157.
- Halperin, David M, 1993. "Is there a history of sexuality?" in: *The Lesbian and Gay Studies Reader*, eds. Henry Abelove, Michele Aina Barale and David M. Halperin, New York: Routledge, pp. 416-426.

- Hartman, Tova, 2002. *Appropriately Subversive: Modern Mothers in Traditional Religions*, Cambridge: Harvard University Press.
- Hequembourg, Amy, 2012. *Lesbian Motherhood: Stories of Becoming*, New-York: Routledge.
- Hetherington, E. Mavis, Henderson, Sandra H., Reiss, David, Anderson, Edward R., Bridges, Margaert, Chan Raymond W., Insabella, Glendessa M., Jodi, Kathleen M., Kim, Jungmeen E, Mitchell, Anne S., O'Connor, Thomas G., Skaggs, Monica J, and Taylor, Lorraine C, 1999. "Adolescent siblings in stepfamilies: Family functioning and adolescent adjustment, *Monographs of the Society for Research in Child Development* 64(4): 1-22.
- Hill Collins, Patricia, 1991. *Black Feminist Thought*, New York & London: Routledge.
  – 1994. "Shifting the center: Race, class and Feminist theorizing about motherhood," in: *Mothering: Ideology, Experience and Agency*, eds. Evelyn Nakano Glenn, Grace Chang and Linda Rennie Forcey, New- York: Routledge, pp. 45-65.
- Human rights, sexual orientation and gender identity, 2011. United Nations General Assembly, A/HRC/RES/17/ 19, July 15, 2011.
- Jack, Dana Crowley, 1991. *Silencing the self: Women and depression*, Cambridge, MA: Harvard University Press.
- Jagose, Annamarie, 1996. *Queer Theory – An Introduction*, New York: New York University Press.
- Jordan, Lee, 2009. "'This is normal for us': Resiliency and resistance amongst lesbian and gay parents," *Gay & Lesbian Issues and Psychology Review* 5(2): 70-80.
- Kadish, Ruti, 2005. "Israeli lesbians, national identity and motherhood," in: *Sappho in the Holy Land: Lesbian Existence and Dilemmas in Contemporary Israel*, eds. Chava Frankfort-Nachmias and Erella Shadmi, New York: State University of New York Press, pp. 223-250.
- King, Beverly R., and Black, Kathryn N., 1999. "Extent of relational stigmatization of lesbians and their children by heterosexual college students," *Journal of Homosexuality* 37(2): 65-81.
- Kranz Karen C., and Daniluk, Judith C., 2002. "We've come a long way baby... or have we? Contextualizing lesbian motherhood in North America," *Journal of the Association for Research on Mothering* 4(1): 58-69.
- Kuvalanka, Katherine A., and Goldberg, Abbie E., 2009. "'Second Generation' voices: Queer youth with lesbian/bisexual mothers," *Journal of Youth and Adolescence* 38(7): 914-919.
- MacCallum, Fiona, and Golombok, Susan, 2004. "Children raised in fatherless families from infancy: A follow-up of children of lesbian and single heterosexual mothers at early adolescence," *Journal of Child Psychology and Psychiatry* 45(8): 1407-1419.

- Mann, Bonnie, 2007. "The lesbian June Cleaver: Heterosexism and Lesbian Mothering," *Hypatia* 22(1): 149-166.
- Masci, David, Sciupac, Elizabeth, and Lipka, Michael, 2019. *Gay marriage around the world*, Washington, DC: Pew Research Center.
- Meyer, Ilan H., 1995. Minority stress and mental health in gay men, *Journal of Health and Social Behavior* 36(1): 38-56.
  – 2003. "Prejudice, social stress and mental health in lesbian, gay and bisexual populations: Conceptual issues and research evidence" *Psychological Bulletin* 129 (5): 674-697.
  – 2016. "Does an improved social environment for sexual and gender minorities have implications for a new minority stress research agenda?" *Psychology of Sexualities Review* 7(1): 81-90.
- O'Reilly, Andrea, 2004. *Mother Outlaws: Theories and Practices of Empowered Mothering*, Virginia: Women's Press.
  – *Feminist Mothering*, Albany: State University of New York Press.
- Patterson, Charlotte J., 1992. "Children of Lesbian and Gay Parents," *Child Development* 63 (5): 1025-1042.
- Patterson, Charlotte J., 1995. "Lesbian mothers, gay fathers and their children," in: *Lesbian, Gay, and Bisexual Identities over the Lifespan: Psychological Perspectives*, eds. Anthony R. D'Augelli and Charlotte J. Patterson, New York: Oxford University Press, pp. 262-290.
- Patterson, Charlotte J., Hurt, Susan, and Mason, Chandra D., 1998. "Families of the lesbian baby boom: Children's contact with grandparents and other adults," *American Journal of Orthopsychiatry* 68(3): 390-399.
- Pachankis, Jhon E., 2007. "The psychological implications of concealing a stigma: A cognitive-affective-behavioral model," *Psychological Bulletin* 133(2): 328-345.
- Peleg, A., & Hartman, T. (2019). Minority stress in an improved social environment: Lesbian mothers and the burden of proof. journal of GLBT Family Studies, 15 (5), 442- 460
- Pelka, Suzanne, 2009. "Sharing Motherhood: Maternal Jealousy Among Lesbian Co-Mothers," *Journal of Homosexuality* 56 (2): 195-217.
- Perlesz, Amaryll, 2005. "Deconstructing the fear of father absence," *Journal of Feminist Family Therapy* 16 (3): 1-29.
- Pies, Cheri A., 1990. "Lesbians and the Choice to Parent," in: *Homosexuality and Family Relations*, eds. Frederick W. Bozzet and Marvin B. Sussman, New York: Routledge, pp.138-153.
- Pridmore-Brown, Michele, 2008. "Professional women, timing and reproductive strategies," in: *Feminist Mothering*, ed. Andrea O'Reilly, Albany: State University of New York Press, pp. 25-43.
- Quinn, Diane M., and Chaudoir, Stephenie R., 2009. "Living with a concealable stigmatized identity: The impact of anticipated stigma,

centrality, salience and cultural stigma on psychological distress and health," *Journal of personality and social psychology* 97(4): 634-651.

- Remennick, Larissa, 2000. "Childless in the land of imperative motherhood: Stigma and coping among infertile Israeli women," *Sex Roles* 43(11/12): 821-840.
- Rivers, Ian, Poteat, Paul V., and Noret, Nathalie, 2008. "Victimization, social support and psychosocial functioning among children of same-sex and opposite-sex couples in the United Kingdom," *Developmental Psychology* 44: 127-134.
- Root, Maria P., 1992. "Reconstructing the impact of trauma on personality," in: *Personality and Psychopathology: Feminist Reappraisals*, eds. Laura S. Brown and Mary Ballou, NY: Guilford Publication, pp. 229-266.
- Rosenthal, Gabriele, 1993. "Reconstruction of life stories: Principles of selection in generating stories for narrative interviews," in: *The Narrative Study of Lives (Volume 1)*, eds. Ruthellen Josselson and Amia Lieblich, Thousand Oaks, CA: Sage publications, pp. 59-91.
- Ross, Michael W., 1985. "Actual and anticipated societal reaction to homosexuality and adjustment in two societies," *The Journal of Sex Research* 21 (1): 40-55.
- Ruddick, Sara, 1989. *Maternal Thinking: Toward a Politics of Peace*, Boston: Beacon Press.
  – 2005. "Maternal Thinking," in: *Maternal Theory: Essential Readings*, ed.
- Andrea O'Reilly, Bradford, Canada: Demeter Press, pp. 96- 113.
- Schnitzer, Phoebe Kazdin, 1998. "He needs his father: The clinical discourse and politics of single mothering," in: *Mothering Against the Odds: Diverse Voices of Contemporary Mothers*, eds. Cynthia Garcia Coll, Janet. L. Surrey and Kathy Weingarten, New York: The Guilford Press, pp. 151-172.
- Shadmi, Erella, 2005. "The construction of lesbianism as a non-issue in Israel." in: *Sappho in the Holy Land*, eds. Chava Frankfort – Nachmias and Erella Shadmi, New York: State University of New York Press, pp.251-267.
- Shapiro, Danielle N., Peterson, Christopher, and Stewart, Abigail J., 2009. "Legal and social contexts and mental health among lesbian and heterosexual mothers," *Journal of Family Psychology* 23(2): 255-262.
- Shildo, Ariel, 1994. "Internalized homophobia: Conceptual and empirical issues in measurement," in: *Lesbian and Gay Psychology: Theory, research and clinical implications*, eds. Beverly Greene & Gregory M. Herek, Thousand Oaks, CA: Sage Publications, pp. 176-205.
- Silverstein, Louise B., and Auerbach, Carl F., 1999. "Deconstructing the essential father," *American Psychologist* 54(6): 1-29.
- Spector-Mersel, Gabriela, 2011. "Mechanisms of selection in claiming narrative identities: A model for interpreting narratives," *Qualitative inquiry* 17(2): 172-185.

- Tasker, Fiona and Golombok, Susan, 1995. "Adults raised as children in lesbian families," *American Journal of Orthopsychiatry* 65(2): 203-215.
- Thurer, Sherry, 1994. *The Myths of Motherhood: How Culture Invents the Good Mother*, New York: Penguin Books.
- Van Gelderen, Loes, Bos, Henny M.W., Gartrell, Nanette, Hermanns, Jo, and Perrin, Ellen C., 2012. "Quality of life of adolescents raised from birth by lesbian mothers: the US national longitudinal family study," *Journal of developmental and behavioral pediatrics* 33(1): 17-23.
- Wells, Jess, 2001. "Lesbians raising sons: Bringing up a new breed of men," in: *Mothers and Sons: Feminism, Masculinity and the Struggle to Raise our Sons*, ed. Andrea O'Reilly, New York: Routledge, pp.154-160.
- Welsh, Marjorie G., 2011."Growing up in a same-sex parented family: The adolescent voice of experience," Journal of GLBT Family Studies 7(1-2): 49-71.
- Williamson, Iain R., 2000. "Internalized homophobia and health issues affecting lesbians and gay men," *Health Education Research* 15 (1): 97-107.
- Winnicott, Donald Woods, 1973. *The Child, the Family, and the Outside World*, London: Penguin books.

Dr. Alona Peleg

References (Hebrew)

- Amir, M. (2008). Lo rak ga'a'va: ha'busha basi'ah hak'wiri [When Pride is Not Enough: Shame in Queer Discourse]. *Teoria ve'bikoret [Theory and criticism]*, 32, 143-153.
- Anzaldúa, G. (2012). *Borderlands/La Frontera: The New Mestiza* (4th ed.). Aunt Lute Books. (Original work published 1987).
- Avni, G. (2015). Takdim: tsav horut lezug lesbiyot bli taskir shel she'rutey ha'revaha [Precedent: Parenting Order for Lesbian Couples without Social Services Report]. *Mako.*
- Baum, D. (2006). Hakdama la'ma'amar shel Ritz Adrian: hetro'seksu'ali'yut kfuya ve'ha'kiyum ha'lesbi [Introduction to Adrienne Rich's article: "Compulsory Heterosexuality and Lesbian Existence]." In D. Amir, Y. Berlovitz, R. Brayer-Garb, et al. (Eds.) *Lilmod Feminism: mikra'a [Learning Feminism: a Reader* 165-166. Hakibbutz Hameuchad.
- Ben David, L. (2009). Hakara mishpatit be'yahasey zugiyut bein bney zug me'oto min – Skira mashva [Legal recognition of marital relationships between same-sex partners – a Comparative Review]. *Mercaz Ha'Mehkar Ve'Hameida shel Ha'Knesset.*
- Berkovitch, N. (1999). Eshet hail mi yimtza? nashim ve'ez'rahut be'Yisra'el [Woman of valor, who will find? Women and Israeli citizenship]. *Sotzio'logya Yisra'elit [Israeli Sociology]*, 1(277-319).
- Butler, J. (1993). Critically Queer. *GLQ, 1*(1), 17-32. https://doi.org/10.1215/10642684-1-1-17
  – (1991). Imitation and gender insubordination. In D. Fuss (Ed.) Inside/Out (1, 13-31).
  – (1990). Gender Trouble: Feminism and the Subversion of Identity. Routledge.
  – (2000). Antigone's Claim: Kinship Between Life and Death. Cambridge University Press.
- Chodoro, N. (1978). *The Reproduction of Mothering: Psychoanalysis and the Sociology of Gender.* University of California Press.
- Dahan-Kalev, H. (2000). Nashim mizrahiot: zehut shel eda ve'migdar ba'hinukh [Mizrahi Women: Ethnic and Gender Identity in Education]. In S. Shlasky (Ed.) *Mini'yut ve'migdar ba'hinuch* [Sexuality and Gender in Education]. Ramot.

- Davidov, E. (2011). *Ta'asu lanu neched* [Make us a grandchild]. *Ynet*.
- Ettinger, Y. (2010). *Asrot rabanim gibshu mis'makh ekronot ha'kore le'hakir be'homo'im ve'lesbiyot* [Dozens of Orthodox rabbis drafted principles document calling for recognition of homosexuals]. *Haaretz*, 1-9.
- Ettinger, Y. (2016). *"Neum hasotim" ma'amik et ha'sdakim ba'tziyonut hadatit* [The "speech of the deviants" deepens cracks in religious Zionism]. *Haaretz*, 5.
- Fanon, F. (2008). *Black Skin, White Masks*. (R. Philcox, Trans) (revised ed.). Grove Press. (Original work published 1952).
- Fogiel-Bijaoui, S. (1999). Mishpahot be'Yisrael: bein mishpahti'yut le post-moderni'yut [Families in Israel: Between Family and Postmoderni-ty]. In D. Izraeli, A. Friedman, H. Dahan-Kalev, H. Herzog, M. Hasan, H. Naveh, S. Fogiel-Bijaoui (Eds.). *Min, migdar, politika, [Sex, Gender, Politics]* (pp.107-167). Hakibbutz Hameuchad.
- Foucault, M. (1998). *The History of Sexuality I: The Will to Knowledge.* (new ed.) Penguin Books. (Original work published 1978).
- Freud, S. (2002). Kama hashla'khot nafshi'yot al ha'hevdel ha'mini ha'ana'tomi [Some psychological consequences of the anatomical distinction between the sexes In I. Berman & I. Shamir (Eds.)*Mini'yut ve'aha'va [Sexuality and Love]*(pp. 187- 212). (A. Tenenbaum & D. Zinger, Trans.) Am Oved Press.
- Friedman, A. (2007). Ima'hut bir'ii ha'teoria [Motherhood reflected in theory]. In N. Yanay, T. El-Or, O. Lubin, and H. Naveh (Eds.). *Drakhim le'hashiva feminstit – mavo le'limudey migdar [Venues of Feminist Thinking: An Introduction to Gender Studies]* (pp. 189-243). The Open University.
- Friedson, Y, Tvizer, I, Porat, Y, & Fox, N. (2019). Alafim bemitz'ad Ha-ga'ava bi'Yru'sha'la'yim, 49 ukvu le'hakira [Thousands at Jerusalem Pride Parade, 49 Detained for Interrogation]. *Ynet*.
- Glazer, H. (2017). Ima, aba ve'haver shel aba: ekh nir'im ha'hayim be'mishpahot had-miniyot be'Yisra'el? [Mom, dad and dad's boyfriend: How does life look for same-sex families in Israel?]. *Haaretz*.
- Gross, E, & Ziv, A. (2003). Bein teo'ria le'praktika: limudim homo-lesbim ve'teo'ria kwirit [Between Theory and Politics: Gay and Lesbian Studies and Queer Theory] In Y. Kedar, A. Ziv & O. Kenner (Eds.) *Me'ever la'mini-yut : mivhar ma'a'marim be'limudim homo-lesbim ve'te'oria kwirit [Beyond Sexuality – A selection of essays in Gay and Lesbian Studies and Queer Theo-ry]*. Hakibbutz Hameuchad.
- Gvirtz, N. (2010). Mehkar: be'mishpa'hot lesbiyot yesh 0% mikrey hit'ale'lut [Study: Lesbian families have 0% cases of abuse]. *Mako*.
- Haaretz Service. (2009). Haim hata ha'mishpa'hti ha'lesbi tov yoter liy'ladim? [Is the lesbian family unit better for children?]. *Haaretz*.

- Hefetz-Schwartz, R. (2010). Yaldey lesbiyot ba'aley bita'hon atzmi rav yoter [Children of lesbians – have more self-confidence]. *Mako.*
- Ilany, O. (2009). Seker Ha'aretz: 46% me'hatzi'bur ro'im be'homo'seksu'alim sotim ["Haaretz survey": 46% of Israelis Think Homosexuals are Deviants]. *Haaretz.*
- Kusharek, N. (2010). Gideon Sa'ar ba'atze'ret bimlot shana la'retzah ba'bar-no'ar: gibashnu tokhnit limudim hadasha le'kabalat ha'a'her [Gideon Sa'ar at the rally marking one year since the murder in Bar-Noar: We formulated a new curriculum for accepting the other. *Haaretz.*
- Kyzer, L. (2010). 3000 tza'a'du be'mitz'ad Ha'ga'va bi'Yru'sha'la'yim: tzeira hutkefa [3000 marched in Jerusalem Pride Parade; Young woman attacked.] *Haaretz.*
- Levi, G. (2010). Haim horut had-minit poga'at ba'yeled? [Does same-sex parenting harm children?]. *Ynet.* www.ynet.co.il/articles/0,7340,L-3846124,00.html
- Lieblich, A. (2003). *Seder nashim: sipurey nashim ba'mishpa'ha ha'hada'sha be'Yisra'el [Women's Code: Stories of Women in the New Family in Israel].* Schocken.
- – (2009). Seder nashim; imahot had-hori'yot mib'hira be'Yisra'el [Women's Code: Single mothers by choice in Israel]. In E. Perroni (Ed.) *Imahoot – mabat me'ha'psikho-ana'liza umi'makom aher [Motherhood: Psychoanalysis and Other Disciplines],* (pp. 214-229). Van Leer Foundation. Hakibbutz Hameuchad
- Lior, I. (2014). Te'udot zehut mat'imot yun'peku li'yla'dim shel zugot had-mini'yim [Israel Tweaks ID cards to account for same-sex parents]. *Haaretz,* p. 6
- – (2015). Be'ikvot ha'psika be'Artzot Habrit. Agudat Ha'la'ha'tab: na'ator le'Bagatz le'ishur nisu'im had- mini'yim [Following U.S. ruling, LGBTQ Association: We will petition the Supreme Court to approve same-sex marriage]. *Haaretz,* p. 3.
- Liss, J, & Skop,Y. (2016). 25,000 tza'a'du bi'Yru'sha'la'yim be'mifgan neged sin'aa ve'homo'fobia [Over 25,000 marched in the Jerusalem pride parade in a demonstration against hate and homophobia]. *Haaretz.*
- Livni, T. (2004). *Horut be'de'rekh lo slula: ima'hut lesbit ba'hevra ha'Yis'ra'elit [Parenting on an Unpaved Road: Lesbian Motherhood in Israeli Society]* Master's thesis. Haifa University.
- Luz, D, & Avni, S. (2000). *Ima, yesh li mashe'hu le'saper lakh [Mom, I've got something to tell you].* Shufra.
- Meir, Y. (2008). *Ima yesh rak a'hat (... o shta'yim): ha'kesher bein lahatz shel mi'utim ve'resha'tot tmikha hevratit le'histaglut psikho'logit ve'horit be'mish'pahot had-miniyot ve'had-horiyot be'Yisra'el ["There's only one (... or two) moms": The relationship between minority stress and social support*

networks and psychological and parental adjustment in same-sex and single-parent families in Israel] Master's thesis. Tel Aviv University.

- Or, Y. (2000). *Hashva'a shel ha'kesher ha'zugi ve'hatif'kud ha'hori bekerev zugot hetro'seksu'alim ve'zugot lesbiyot [Comparing marital relationships and parental functioning among heterosexual and lesbian couples],* Master's thesis. Bar-Ilan University, Ramat Gan.

- Patterson, C. (1995). Sikum mem'tzaey meh'karim al horut lesbit ve'ho-mo'seksu'alit [Summary of study's findings: Lesbian and homosexual parenting]. In D. Baum & I. Maran (Eds.) *Lesbi'yut ve'homo'seksuali'yut bir'ii ha'metziut – asufat ma'a'marim Lesbianism and Homosexuality Reflected in Reality – A Collection of Essays],* (pp. 39-48). Kehila Lesbit Feministit (KLaF).

- Perroni, E. (2009). Mavo – ima'hut ve'ima'hi'yut [Introduction – Motherhood and Motherness]. In E. Perroni (Ed.) *Ima'hut – mabat me'ha'psikho-ana'liza umi'makom aher [Motherhood: Psychoanalysis and Other Disciplines],* (pp. 9-19). Van Leer Foundation: Hakibbutz Hameuchad

- Palgi-Hecker, A. (2005). *Me'ii-mahut le'ima'hut: hipus psikho-analiti feminsti a'har ha'em ke'subyekt [From No Essence to Motherhood: A feminist psychoanalytic search for the mother as a subject].* Am Oved.

- Rich, A. (2003). Compulsory heterosexuality and lesbian existence. *Journal of Women's History, 15*(3), 11-48.
  – (2021). *Of Woman Born.* WW Norton & Co. (6th ed.)

- Rivi, E. (1999). *Ta'halikh "ha'ye'tzia me'ha'aron" shel mit'bagrot lesbiyot Yis'ra'eliyot: me'af'yenim ve'dfusey hit'mode'dut [The "coming out" process of Israeli lesbian adolescents: characteristics and coping patterns].* Master's thesis. Haifa University.

- Rozmarin, M. (2010). Antigona, el ma she'me'ever – aha'rit davar [Antigone, towards the beyond – Epilogue]. In Y. Binyamini & I. Tzivoni (Eds.) *Judit Batler – ta'a'nat Anti'gona – ya'hasey she'e'rut bein ha'im le'mavet [Judith Butler – Antigone's Claim: Kinship Between Life and Death]* (pp. 111-133). Resling.

- Shechter, R. (2009). *Hitna'hagut hevra'tit, psikho-patologia vet'fisa atzmit shel yeladim mi'mish'pahot had-miniyot ve'had-horiyot be'Yisra'el [Social behavior, psychopathology and self-perception of children from same-sex and single parent families in Israel].* Master's thesis. Tel Aviv University.

- Shadmi, E. (2007). *La'ha'shov isha: nashim ve'fe'minizm be'hevra gavrit [Thinking as a Woman: Women and Feminism in Israel],* (pp. 106-116). Tziv'onim.

- Shayovitz-Gurman, SH. (2009). *Ambi'valen'tiyut be'hava'yata shel ha'em klapei yaldah: shni'yut ve'shnayim ba'kesher she'bein em va'yeled [Ambivalence in the mother's experience towards her child: Duplication in the mother-child relationship].* Master's thesis. Bar-Ilan University.

- Shilo, G. (2007). *Ha'ha'yim be'varod. Bnei no'ar ve'tze'irim- homo'im, les-biyot, bi'seksu'alim ve'trans'jenderim [Life in Pink. Teens and Young Adults – Gay, Lesbian, Bisexual and Transgender]*. Resling.
  – (2012). Hasipur eino kol ha'sipur: te'hudat ha'zehut ha'nera'tivit [The story is not the whole story: The narrative identity card]. *Megamot, 48*(2), 227-250.
- Triger, Z. (2006). Mish'pahot horgot ve'"rishyon horut": mah'sha'vot al ha'kesher bein hakara baz'khut le'horut ve'bein hakara be'zugi'yut be'ikvot ir'ur ezrahi shel Yaros- Hakak 10280/01 [Stepfamilies and "Parenting License": Thoughts on the Connection between Recognition of the Right to Parenting and Recognition of Partnership Following Civil Appeal 10280/01 Yaros-Hakak v. Attorney General]. *Hamishpat, 22*(44-51).
- Tuval-Mashiach, R, & Spector-Mersel, G. (2010). Mavo klali – meh'kar nerativi – hagdarot ve'hek'sherim [General introduction – Narrative research: Definitions and contexts] In G. Spector-Mersel & R. Tuval-Mashiach (Eds.) *Meh'kar nerativi: te'oria, ye'tzira ve'parsha'nut [Narrative Research: Theory, Creation and Interpretation]*, (pp. 7-34). Magnes Press.
- Tzidkiyahu, G. (2004). *Le'hishta'hot al ha'she'ela hazot – lesbiyot Yis'ra'eli-yot mul hab'hira ve'ha'hakh'ra'a bi'she'elat ha'ima'hut]. [Contemplating the question – Israeli lesbians versus the choice and decision on the question of motherhood]*. Master's thesis. Bar-Ilan University.
- Wittig, M. (2016). One is not born a woman. In C. R. McCann & S.K. Kim (Eds.), *Feminist theory reader* (4th ed.). Routledge. (Original work published 1981).
- Zellermayer, M. (2010). Al meh'kar nerativi, al feminizm ve'al ma she'beine'hem [About narrative research, feminism and everything in between]. In G. Spector-Mersel & R. Tuval-Mashiach (Eds.) – *Meh'kar nerativi: te'oria, ye'tzira ve'parsha'nut [Narrative Research: Theory, Creation and Interpretation]*, (pp. 106-132). Magnes Press.
- Ziv, A. (2007). Judit batler: tzarot shel migdar [Judith Butler: Gender Trouble]. In N. Yanay, T. El-Or, O. Lubin, & H. Naveh (Eds.), *Drakhim le'hashiva feminstit – mavo le'limudey migdar [Venues of Feminist Thinking: An Introduction to Gender Studies]*, (pp. 619-661). The Open University.
- Ziv, E. (2012). Trauma ikeshet [Insidious trauma]. *Mafte'akh, 5* (74-75).

Made in United States
North Haven, CT
31 January 2025